D0441611

What Pupils Really Think about Their Schools

Also available from Continuum

The SAS Guide to Teaching, Brian Carline
How to Be a Successful Head of Year, Brian Carline
How to Improve Your School, Jean Rudduck and Julia Flutter

What Pupils Really Think about Their Schools

A Powerful Resource for School Improvement

Brian Carline

CONTINUUM

The Tower Building	80 Maiden Lane
11 York Road	Suite 704
London	New York
SE1 7NX	NY 10038

www.continuumbooks.com

© Brian Carline 2008

All rights reserved. No part of this publication may be reproduced or transmitted in any form or by any means, electronic or mechanical, including photocopying, recording or any information storage or retrieval system, without prior permission from the publishers.

Brian Carline has asserted his right under the Copyright, Designs and Patents Act, 1988, to be identified as Author of this work.

British Library Cataloguing-in-Publication Data
A catalogue record for this book is available from the British Library.

ISBN 9781847061072 (paperback)

Library of Congress Cataloging-in-Publication Data
A catalog record for this book is available from the Library of Congress.

Typeset by YHT Ltd, London
Printed and bound in Great Britain by MPG Books Ltd, Cornwall

Contents

To the late Bill Webster. A kind and generous man.
My good friend.

Acknowledgements

I would like to thank the many pupils whose observations and comments have contributed to the compilation of this book. It is a testimony to their uninhibited honesty. I also thank the teachers and parents of these youngsters who have given permission for me to interview them and use their anecdotes and opinions.

I am also grateful to my teaching colleagues for helping me recall remarks made by pupils over a timescale of some forty years. In particular, I am indebted to David Summerville and Rob Woodburn for their lucid memories.

BWC
January 2008

Introduction

The piercing shrill of the bell to signify the end of morning break seemed to cut through the many conversations and general hubbub in the main school corridor. I was just leaving the staffroom as two loquacious Year 9 girls walked by, unimpressed by my presence. The somewhat louder member of the duo enquired of her companion:

> ''Ere, Shell. Are you a virgin?'

The friend, who was in the process of blowing the most successful chewing gum bubble ever, completed the inflation, and out of the corner of her mouth gave the unruffled reply:

> 'Naaa. Not yet.'

In the course of your teaching career you will be privy to much pupil dialogue, opinions and ideas. Not all will involve misnomer and carry the same degree of legitimacy and reliability as our two pubescent gossipmongers'. Indeed, you will hear informed opinion by eavesdrop or during uninhibited, honest and open discussion with pupils. This wealth of perceptions will lead you to the inevitable conclusion that pupils really do have an understanding of what is going on in their schools and that their opinions and experiences too should form part of a prescription for any school improvement programme.

The principal thrust of this book examines why and how we as teachers should listen to a school's clientele and subsequently learn from them about ways of making school life a better experience for everyone. Student participation in decision making and analysis will, for some teachers, have an apocalyptic ring to it and present anxiety and uncomfortable prospects. Some of your colleagues will wish to maintain the 'us and them' relationship and see the terms 'consultation' and 'participation' as the seeds of revolution and anarchy. If the process of student involvement in school improvement starts small and is allowed to grow slowly then the positive rewards of such an initiative will soon become apparent and spawn mutual benefit.

Giving the pupils of a school a voice and a role in decision making will lead to improved school policies and practices. This may engender greater relevance and understanding and reduce the frequency of comments such as:

> 'My English teacher reckons I'm a level 5, though what the 'ell that means, I dunno.'

It will contribute to ways of improving teaching and learning. Pupil feedback on ways of learning, teaching styles and methodologies may help eradicate negative pupil perceptions such as:

> 'That man has completely destroyed my love of science this term.'

Pupil involvement in the development of a new initiative will lead to its more successful implementation. It may, therefore, prevent remarks like:

> 'Anyone could have told 'em that new Toilet Pass card was open to forgery. I ran off 20 on my computer last night. How many do you want?'

Pupil participation in decision making will strengthen the democratic process within the school and will foster improved relationships between students, teachers and the community.

We have come a long way from the Dickensian academies run by Thomas Gradgrind and Wackford Squeers in terms of recognizing the moral and legal imperatives of student participation and decision making. The United Nations Convention on the Rights of The Child (1989) underlines the prerequisite of participation by children and young people in freedom of expression and decision making processes in all matters affecting them.

Consultation with pupils in all aspects of school life has to be genuine. The school council was possibly the first venture into recognizing the need for a student voice. This vehicle met with success in many institutions and was valued by both schools and pupils as an effective way forward for school advancement. However, some school council programmes became unproductive and faced inertia because of a lack of true commitment from teachers.

When young people are asked to say what they think about an issue but know their views will be disregarded, they readily identify such empty participation as tokenism. They also object to being used as decoration when they know their presence in the democratic process is in name only and that matters for debate have not been fully explained to them. Student council members easily detect adults' attempts to manipulate their views and opinions to secure preconceived solutions or decisions.

We should never underestimate our pupils. I have

attended school and year council meetings and been so impressed with the fluency, maturity and wisdom of their student members. Indeed, I have often felt tempted to ask them about undertaking a spell of supply teaching.

Schools can cite many examples of positive changes that have been brought about by pupil consultation and participation. I admired the work of one school council of an inner city school. They invited local councillors into their school to discuss the lack of recreation provision for youths in the locality and the high incidence of youth crime. The Head teacher also arranged for them to speak with the police to support their case. Other local school councils were contacted and asked to work with them.

> 'I think the councillors were taken aback when we made our presentation. They couldn't do anything but agree with us. Our Head said she was dead proud of us. We weren't unreasonable about what we felt should happen and she said that's what did the trick.'

Pupils have also been instrumental in the implementation of campaigns such as 'Safer Journeys to School' and 'Healthy Schools'. School projects to support and enrich learning have also blossomed because of their involvement. Homework clubs, study support sessions and enrichment classes have all come to fruition. Another school reviewed its PSHCE (Personal, Social, Health and Citizenship Education) programme and elected a working party composed of equal numbers of teachers and students to act as its review team.

Some schools have enlisted the participation of their school councils to contribute to the broad remit of looking at their rewards and sanctions. Assembly programmes were the subject of analysis at one establishment which was anxious to improve this corporate daily act. The help of a student council was sought by one pastoral team determined to give pupils more of an identity and promote healthy competition. The result was a house system within a year framework of which both teachers and pupils were proud.

Several intrepid schools have used student opinion to improve the quality of the teaching and learning. This bold move, though contentious to some, is just one way of examining and improving the calibre of classroom services we provide for pupils.

There is much we can learn from our pupils. We can and should involve them in any mission for improving our schools.

Educational change is something that has brought teachers to their knees over the past ten years. Change has been imposed upon us by many whose last visit to a classroom was to collect their A level results. It would be selfish of us to claim that teachers were the only casualties of such protracted and detailed reforms. Our pupils too were forced to shoulder an overdose of changes to testing, National Curriculum, public examinations, recording and assessment. Therefore, I feel it justified that we recognize and listen to this often forgotten voice in education. Education is, after all, a partnership and student opinions, ideas and experience should form part of any blueprint for school improvement.

The following chapters reflect and listen to their honesty.

1 Pupils as individuals

When 10A are sat facing you three periods a week for History, it's sometimes easy to forget about them as people. The pressure you are under to get them through the examination syllabus gives you precious little time to gain in-depth knowledge of them as individuals.

I recall a junior colleague once pleading self-defence when a conscientious Key Stage 4 pupil rebuked him for failing to mark the essay she had handed in the day before:

> 'I do have a life outside of school, you know, Simone. I mean, there are other things for me to do at home than to just mark your essays!'

This flippant and unnecessary remark was undoubtedly due to tiredness and overwork. Nevertheless, if we as teachers expect our students to occasionally empathize and appreciate our personal circumstances, then it's only right for us to be cognizant of their individual backgrounds. Just as we anticipate an understanding from them that we too belong to the species *Homo sapiens*, so should we reciprocate such awareness.

Greater knowledge and understanding of the specific circumstances of pupils can do nothing but improve the school experience we provide for them. It is, therefore, important that we know pupils as individuals and not as a name on a subject register. There are many important differences between pupils and groups of pupils, all of which can have an impact on their lives both in and out of the classroom. Factors such as their family, race, religion, social class, gender, motivation and ability will all influence attitudes and performance in school. Many of these factors are not mutually exclusive and may often overlap.

Parental occupation is the primary determinant of what we call social class. Professional occupations such as doctors and lawyers are clearly regarded as middle class. Manual workers, semi- and unskilled workforces fall into the working class category. Pupils with middle class parents achieve higher educational attainment than their working class counterparts. The principal driving force behind this fact is that middle class parents have higher educational expectations. The theory continues in that middle class homes are likely to provide environments that promote greater intellectual development, motivation to succeed and encourage greater academic self-confidence. Middle class parents also provide a wider range of interests for their children and use language that is in tune with the learning process in schools.

Working class homes, however, are more likely to contain elements that will work against school expectations and limit a child's capacity to shoulder these demands. Factors such as poor housing and poverty are key issues influencing school experience for pupils.

This elementary sociological research into the impact of social class upon a child's education can often give the misguided picture that all is fine in middle class homes and that students who live with their working class parents are always likely to gain less from their time spent at school. The term 'dysfunctional family' can, for example, cut across all social classes from royals through to serfs. The term 'the family' simply means what you find when you knock on the door of the place where the student lives. Today, you will find few conventional textbook family norms. Today, expect any possibility. The potential for diverse family structures and their related dynamics will have an expected impact upon the children. These youngsters will be the pupils you teach. As teachers, we are ready to accept that schools do put pressure on their pupils but what we sometimes overlook are the tensions these young people experience due to circumstances at home.

An eloquent Year 11 student, whose enunciation reminded me of art critic Brian Sewell, spoke of the powerful influence of his father:

> 'My father is an accountant. He has fixed ideas about my schooling and my future. He wants me to read law at university. He's a bit of a bully in most things. Nobody relishes challenging him.'

Another pupil, again from a middle class home, mentioned her parents with great embarrassment:

> 'I suppose you would call my parents "pushy". They first labelled me a sensitive child and then proceeded to inform any teacher they would meet of this fact. I'm quite happy with the way things are working out for me at school but they are always on the phone to my teachers about things. I've told them it's quite humiliating but they don't see it.'

It is sometimes easy to think that a family domiciled in 'The Spinney' or 'Maltings Chase' will have trouble-free children who are model students. This erroneous interpretation ignores the fundamental fact that all parents experience problems with adolescence and that some are better at dealing with them than others. A Year 13 student testified to this fact:

> 'My friends always tease me about where I live. Yes, I suppose it is rather grand. They say the pigeons fly upside down as a mark of respect for our area. Just because my Mum and Dad have got a few bob doesn't mean they're excellent parents. On the contrary, my father drinks too much and tends to shout a lot. My mother has never been good at coping with issues around everyday life.'

An astute member of Year 11 told me of his parent:

> 'My Mum goes on and on about my exams and the amount of work I should be doing. She feels under a lot of pressure to bring us up since my Dad died. I know she means well but it gets on my nerves. Sometimes when she gets worked up and starts crying I try to reduce the tension and say something like, "You'd better be nice to me, Mum, 'cos in a few years' time I've got to decide which home I'm going to put you in." She laughs and wipes away her tears and calls me a cheeky bugger.'

Some children will tell you that they really enjoy coming to school to get away from issues at home. Cramped accommodation, tensions between parents and financial worries can all induce unhappy household scenes. Many teachers have experienced relatively comfortable and untroubled childhoods. It can often come as quite a shock when pupils offload to them some distressing domestic episode. A Year 8 girl told me of her plight and how it impacts on her school life:

> 'The flats where we live are horrible. We've had our names down at the Council for a move, for ages now. It's too squashed for the size of our family. There's nutters who live next door to us playing music at all times of the day and night. The couple above us are smashed most of the time and shout at each other. I come to school to get away from it all. I wish we could move.'

It's also easy to overlook the fact that for some kids, the school dinner, in all its Jamie Oliver guises, is the only substantial nourishment they will receive in that day. Their nutritional supplement will include crisps, fizzy drinks and frequent visits to the chippy. A Year 7 pupil spoke candidly about his gourmet encounters:

> 'Sunday dinner is what I really look forward to. We have a roast and it's blindin'. Rest of the week is make do, really. Me Mam works long hours and me sister is supposed to get the tea. It's mostly pizza or crackin' open a tin o' beans. We have chips a lot.'

It is a horrifying statistic that in the classes you teach, approximately half of these pupils will see their parents separate or divorce during their school years. Split family situations often precipitate their own unique difficulties. Many of these side effects may influence a pupil's attitude, behaviour and performance in school. If we are aware of such changes in the home then we are better prepared for dealing with them. Some potential problems can be pre-empted. Divorce and separation will frequently produce responses from students similar to those who have suffered parental bereavement.

There are families who are extremely sensitive about releasing information relating to changes in family circumstances. Understandably, it is a revelation when you discover the reason for a pupil's slip in performance is parental separation. I recall a response from a pragmatic mother about an enquiry relating to her son's recent deterioration in general demeanour and academic performance:

> 'He's really changed since his Dad cleared off last year. He idolized him. Now he hardly ever sees him. He feels really

> betrayed and let down. Trouble is, he takes it out on me and it also looks as though the school's getting a hard time too!'

Another parent who felt exasperated by her boy's newfound aggressiveness, since the family split, made the humorous yet desperate comment:

> 'I can't do a thing with him at home either. He's become a horrible child. So much so, Mr Carline, I'm tempted not to give him any bus fare in the hope that someone will abduct him on the way home!'

A young teaching colleague reacted with disbelief when a pupil informed him that in her home there was no access to the internet. In fact, the family did not possess a computer. They had a television but her parents could not afford both, not yet, anyway. We should be mindful of the fact that even in the age of benefits and allowances, poverty still exists and causes serious limitations on family circumstances. A student who is reluctant to participate in a school trip or activity may do so for financial reasons. I remain ambivalent about a school's propaganda boasting opportunities for youngsters to take part in expensive tours and pursuits. This can sometimes impose significant financial pressure on parents who wish their children to take advantage of such experiences. One girl told me:

> 'I'd love to have gone on that skiing trip to Italy. Some of my friends were going and we'd have had a great laugh. My parents couldn't afford it. Not this year. We'd have had to go without a family holiday if I'd have gone.'

There was a feeling of equitability about the decision.

Not a hint of resentment, more a sensible empathy and a true understanding of the family position.

A measurable success of any school is the degree of cooperation it shows with parents. Parents are encouraged to act as co-educators and take an active participatory role in the education of their child. Some parents will, understandably, prefer to take a back seat in this process and leave it all to the teachers. Their own school experience may not have been a positive one and they may not provide any support and guidance in any matters relating to school.

> 'My Dad never asks me about school. The only thing he has said is that if any teachers gives me a hard time, he'd go up there and sort 'em out.'

A contrasting, yet still worrying statement relating to GCSE coursework was overheard from a pupil about the degree of parental participation in education:

> 'This Science coursework deadline is impossible. It will take my Mum hours.'

A black Caribbean boy stressed the matriarchal influence in his family:

> 'When it comes to school things, my Dad takes a back seat. It's my Mum who runs the show.'

It has been estimated that more than three hundred languages are spoken by children in London schools, making the capital the most linguistically diverse place in the world. Although English remains overwhelmingly the most common first language, for more than 30 per cent of children it is not the language they will speak or hear at home. Languages ranging from Bengali to Vietnamese are spoken in the home and English may be just one of a range of second language possibilities. Information leaflets found in schools in inner city areas now include languages as familiar as Sylheti and the less common Farsi.

Anecdotal evidence suggests that in families where English is spoken as the second language, either there are high levels of unemployment, or parents work at a level below their qualification, experience or potential. One Punjabi girl told me:

> 'My parents do not speak English well. My Dad is doing a qualification in communication skills but he went for a job and they insisted on an NVQ level 3. He's a clever man but he's had to take a job as a cleaner in an office to bring some money into our home.'

Families with English as the second language are more likely to experience poverty than their native English-speaking counterparts.

According to the 2003 census, in secondary schools, four out of five pupils still fit the description 'white British'. Asians from the Indian subcontinent form the second largest ethnic group in schools. Indians outnumber Pakistanis and there are approximately equal numbers of African and black Caribbean pupils.

It is unfortunate that some teachers continue to have very different expectations of pupils from different ethnic groups and that there is still some form of unintentional labelling. Low achievement from black Caribbean and Pakistani boys and high expectations of Asian girls can become self-fulfilling prophecies if these ideas are internalized by the pupils affected. A black

Year 11 student, whose parents came to the UK from St Kitts, explained:

> 'OK, I know I was a pain in Years 7 to 9. I had problems with settling into the area and the school. But I've changed now and I want a good job. I think some teachers expect me to fail.'

A black Caribbean Year 10 boy, about to embark on a period of work experience, made the following prophetic remark to his tutor:

> 'When I go to fast food shops, garages or supermarkets, if anything gets spilled on the floor it's always a black bloke who wipes up the mess. It don't exactly fill me with hope being placed in a pizza parlour, Miss!'

Another comment concerning expectations was made by a teacher to a parent of a Chinese girl at a consultation evening:

> 'We find all Chinese girls do well in our school, Mr Lau. They have a strong work ethic.'

I overheard another rather thoughtless remark made by a teacher over a coffee at morning break:

> 'I mean, I don't actually teach him but he tells me his Mum speaks Yoruba at home. He has quite a strong accent. He must struggle in English lessons.'

The extent of ESOL (English Spoken as Other Language) teaching in schools is once more influenced by budgets. Some students engaged in such lessons have indicated they would prefer more systematic teaching and a curriculum with not only an educational context but also topics exploring home life and occupational dimensions.

By law, collective worship in British schools still has to be 'broadly Christian' in focus. This requirement forms part of the menu of the National Curriculum. It is most encouraging that many schools use this time to foster religious ecumenism and that festivals such as Diwali and Rosh Hashanah now seem less of a mystery to the school population. It is also essential for us to remember when these religious festivals take place. Ramadan, for example, occupies the ninth month on the Muslim calendar and is thus not a fixed date on Western equivalents. Thirty days of fasting for the daylight hours by young Muslims can have serious implications for concentration and stamina during the school day. A talented Year 11 sportsman spoke very fondly and positively about his PE teacher:

> 'Sir changes the PE activities we do during Ramadan. He knows the Muslim boys in our group. He doesn't push us hard at all and there's always water at hand.'

A rather dejected Year 10 girl told me of her alienation by some of her year group when she was instructed by her parents not to attend rehearsals for the drama production after school. The girl was a Seventh Day Adventist and her Sabbath commenced on Friday evening.

> 'I had not told my friends of our religious beliefs until now. They found it hard to understand the reason why I couldn't be there. I'm sure they thought I was making it up. One of them said that if her Dad put pressure on her like that she'd tell him where to go!'

It is hardly stop-press news that gender has an impact on the behaviour and academic performance of secondary school pupils. We are constantly reminded that girls outperform boys at GCSE, girls mature earlier than boys, boys seem less organized and conscientious and that boys are more aggressive than girls. The stories continue with boys being more susceptible to peer group pressure, acknowledging finer feelings less and appearing more sceptical and questioning. There is a danger that these generalizations could lead to teachers making wrong predictions about the likely achievements of particular students. The issue of gender stereotyping has been made clear to pupils by the way that some teachers are seen to operate.

> 'He goes mental at me when I start talking but when she does it he's nice-y, nice-y.'

> 'It seems it's one rule for them [the girls] and one for us [the boys]. She picks on us.'

Taking further the preconception that boys conform to a stereotype, some teachers say they anticipate boys misbehaving, dominating class discussion and making rude and disparaging remarks to girls and female staff. A Year 9 boy defended his gender by highlighting the behaviour of some of the girls in his group:

> 'There's three girls in particular in our Science group. They're really disruptive and mess about. Our teacher can't really control them. He doesn't seem to be good at dealing with girls.'

A girl in Year 10 told me about her concerns for the GCSE examinations:

> 'I think it's a "confidence thing" with me. I work hard and get there in the end. The boys in our group are really cocky about their work and if they don't do well in tests they always say it's 'cos they didn't revise. I know some of them did.'

Many pupils recognize the work done by their schools concerning equal opportunity issues. Girls more than boys commented on the equal opportunity topics they covered in PSHCE and assembly programmes. Girls more than boys identified the display work in subject areas that featured material on equal opportunities relating to gender. A rather macho Year 11 boy, sensitive to injustice but conceptually lame, commented on his Head of Year's efforts to raise achievement in a group of underperforming boys:

> 'I don't need this tracking business. I notice he don't do it with the girls. Now that's sexual harassment in anyone's book.'

Girls mature and reach puberty before boys and there will always be those boys who are late developers. These individuals find it difficult to compete with the rest of the group. They may be poor sportsmen or fighters. These individuals suffer low self-esteem and can often develop other 'skills' to make them more popular. Naughty behaviour in class is just one of their compensatory methods. One Year 10 girl appeared quite bored with a male member of her Maths group:

> 'Godwil is so immature. He's always making silly remarks and messing around. He's quite disruptive, really. I think he's even becoming a bit of a pain with some of the boys. Our teacher isn't very good at controlling him so my friend Letitia often gives him a whack.'

Allowing pupils access to help and guidance relating to their personal development was seen as an important role to be played by the school. The PSHCE classes touched on many of these issues but many students said they would welcome greater access to counselling and support services. The role of the school nurse was considered by many to be a helpful resource for providing information and advice on weight watching, skin care and issues concerning sexual health. The new, wider role of the Connexions service was used by a limited and select group of students. Having access to a school counsellor was seen as a tremendous step forward. They were viewed as neutral sources of support and guidance, halfway between school and home.

Teachers spend their pensionable years in a diverse selection of schools. Some establishments I would class as frontier schools where life is so tough they employ their own coroner. Other places are less like Fort Apache but where the average life expectancy of its teaching staff is still less than a naked man standing inside a nuclear reactor. There are those in our ranks who will work in the more tranquil classrooms of the independent sector.

It doesn't matter if it's a comprehensive in Salford or a private school in Richmond upon Thames, teachers will complain about the kids they teach. It's a directive in their job description. They exercise this right as early as their baptismal weeks of teaching practice and hone this skill until the day they retire. You may have just had the mother of a week and be tempted to sell matches on a street corner. The one thing we must never forget, however, is that we deal with pupils who have identities and responsibilities at home as well as at school. Some of their domestic and social obligations will engender nothing but total respect from us. These youngsters will have to not only shoulder academic pressure but also cope with what society throws at them. Peer pressure and the media will sometimes force them to make potentially life-changing choices on whether to take drugs, to binge drink, to smoke and to participate in unprotected sex.

Some pupils will show an experience of life and a maturity that compels us to value their views and opinions. It was the following words from a pensive Year 11 pupil that reinforced my support for pupil voice:

> 'You see, Sir, we have the most to lose when our schools aren't working right and the most to gain when they are.'

A summary of what the pupils say

1 We'd like teachers to remember that we too are people who have lives outside school and that we have other responsibilities.
2 We don't want to be labelled or stereotyped just because of the occupation of our parents.
3 Don't think that just because we live in a 'posh' area that our lives are problem free.
4 Don't think that just because we live at an address like Flat 254, Mussolini Tower on the Dictators' Council Estate that our families are dysfunctional.
5 We'd like you to appreciate that we all experience problems with life at home and that sometimes they will affect our lives at school.
6 Sometimes we are up against the attitudes of our parents concerning school matters.
7 Some of our parents are 'mentalists' and unreasonable about our work–life balance. We'd like the

school to give them honest and practical information about this topic.

8 We'd like all teachers to realize that poverty does still exist in the UK. Many of our families do have serious money worries. Offering expensive school trips can sometimes put our families under even more financial pressure.
9 Circumstances at home can sometimes affect our ability to complete coursework or homework and sometimes it may be difficult for us to talk about them.
10 Many of us will unfortunately experience our parents separating or divorcing. This may affect our feelings and attitudes. We appreciate it may not be great for you but it is certainly no Garden of Eden for us either.
11 Many of us do not speak English at home. English may be our second language.
12 Don't label us in terms of expectations because of our ethnic group.
13 We applaud the conscious work done by our schools that reflects the multicultural society in which we live.
14 We'd like our schools to build on the work done by student councils. We don't want to control schools but just to be allowed to voice how we feel schools can be improved.
15 We too would like to be involved in solving the mystery of underachieving boys.

2 Teaching and learning (1)

It must be rather disconcerting for any teacher who is halfway through their first term with a class, during the course of a lesson, to ask the well-intentioned question

> 'Can everyone hear me at the back, by the way?'

and eventually to receive an anaemic and reluctant 'Yes' from only two members of the rear cohort. It's even more significant and unsettling when they also detect the whisper of the word 'unfortunately'.

Whenever you join a school and wish to know the names of its good classroom practitioners, the pupils will be able to tell you. They are on the receiving end of our classroom craft and performance and have their own ideas about what constitutes effective teaching. They know the basic characteristics of a good lesson. They know when they have learned something. They know, therefore, when learning is a pleasure.

Were you to probe the reasons why individuals fall into such an exclusive category of good teaching, you would receive a number of common descriptors dressed with a wide ranging vocabulary. Some of their recognition of talent needs careful translation. If someone is depicted as

> 'Her lessons are mint. Well good!'

or

'He's the dog's. Wicked!'

that person should be flattered and should consider remaining in the job. Comments involving the term 'crap' are pretty self-evident and will obviously apply to those at an uncertain stage in their teaching career.

If we distil the verbiage from our classroom pundits then we invariably find about six common criteria. Children prefer teachers who are:

1 slightly strict but not over-severe or permissive;
2 fair and consistent in their use of rewards and punishments;
3 able to treat pupils as individuals;
4 approachable, good humoured and not sarcastic;
5 able to explain things clearly and have a good knowledge of their subject;
6 able to make lessons interesting and provide a variety of stimulating work.

(Wragg et al., *Class Management in the Secondary School*, Routledge Farmer, 2000)

The new-look *Times Educational Supplement* with its colourful magazine includes a weekly article called 'My best teacher', always penned by some celebrity or icon. The contributors regularly gush with affection and nostalgia about their chosen figure and seem to use common descriptive language. After trawling through about a dozen accounts of these avuncular heroes of pedagogy, I decided to put pen to paper and urge the *TES* to publish a one-off feature 'Common adjectives used to describe your best teacher'. The terms 'inspirational', 'enthusiastic', 'stimulating', 'encouraging', 'influential' and 'motivational' would then suitably replace five thousand pages of idolatry and save a copse somewhere in Sweden.

The most important factor cited by students as unhelpful to teaching and learning is bad behaviour. There is an expectation from these students that you, the classroom teacher, will prevent such unacceptable conduct and maintain order in the classroom. Students also see it as the school's responsibility to 'sort out' disruptive pupils and employ a number of sanctions so that effective learning can take place. They do not, for example, see it as unreasonable to split up disruptive kids and even exclude those who constantly disturb the class and make learning difficult. However, their innate desire to speak out is too frequently repressed by those pupils who would seek to intimidate anyone who dares to offer criticism. There is, therefore, a feeling among pupils that there is little peer group cachet to be gained from such radical punitive suggestions. On the occasions when poor pupil behaviour is underlined at student council, many members feel rather let down when they are informed of the limited sanctions that are available to a school.

Whenever a teacher assumes the reins of a new class the pupils openly admit they try to suss you out and test you on a number of issues. They wish to see how much latitude you will allow them. Are you an 'easy touch' or soft? They must discover this in the initial hours of your teaching your subject. They report that the first few meetings you have with the group and the way you set out your stall for the year enables them to place you in a particular classification group – 'good teacher', 'poor teacher' or 'should try a career as a traffic warden, teacher'.

Pupils say that they prefer core routines and a code of behaviour established during your initial sessions with the group, because at least they know where they stand. Consistency of approach applies to both disciplinary and reward issues and they see it as the key to the way you treat them. One Year 7 student commented:

> 'Miss spent most of the first lesson explaining what she wanted from us. She even had us lined up in silence outside the classroom. Her talk was about how she wanted us to learn things and how we are to behave during the year. She seemed strict and soon sorted out Lee Aspinell.'

In your aim to impose a controlled learning environment the pupils want you to be firm but fair. Kids do not respond well to repressive regimes and say this damages rather than helps the learning process. One Year 10 pupil described his History teacher as 'The Robert Mugabe of Merseyside' because he constantly attempts to subjugate his group.

They see us make mistakes in our management of behaviour when we teach. If you are drawn into arguments or confrontations with pupils then this behaviour is viewed by them as a serious error. One Year 9 girl said:

> 'I don't know why he's even bothered trying to argue with Lisa. She's far better at arguing than him. She always wins.'

Another rather perceptive member of the same year commented:

> 'Lisa always picks a fight with him. Ain't he seen "Lauren" on *The Catherine Tate Show* on the tele? It's just like that. She leads him from one thing to another. When he tells her off about chewing it eventually finishes up in an argument about something nothing to do with eating in class.'

Remember, your role is not to allow a situation to escalate. Don't make majors out of minors. Reduce tension rather than fuel it. Sometimes it's far better for you to see certain recalcitrants on their own rather than on the public stage. You can be assured of not losing face by this approach. In fact, if you are a good disciplinarian, and respected for your classroom practice, then kids prefer any admonishment to take place behind closed doors.

It does not do your classroom credibility any good if, in the heat of the moment, you say impossible things to pupils. Your audience remembers your public challenge and you may have to back down.

> 'I thought you was going to get Siobhan permanently excluded from your lesson, Miss?'

This is an embarrassing question to answer when Siobhan continues to sit on the back row for the rest of the year.

Pupils have indicated that some teachers openly court poor behaviour in their lessons because of their naïvety and inexperience. Staff who turn their backs on a group for too long are seen to invite trouble. Similarly, teachers who leave the room are really lighting serious touchpaper. One Year 13 student, who had passed a classroom where the teacher was in the corridor speaking to an LSA (Learning Support Assistant), was heard to tell a fellow member of his year:

> 'He [the teacher] seemed quite oblivious to the mayhem taking place in his classroom. The kids were all over the place, up the walls, on the chairs. It was like a good night at The Hacienda.'

Some aspects of body language too can upset pupils. Excessive finger pointing, eyeballing and being in someone's face all receive 'nul points' from your flock. If your style is to point more than a bricklayer and converse like Hannibal Lecter then you may be in the wrong job.

There will be many golden rules about classroom management that you will learn by the mistakes you make with pupils. I cannot emphasize enough the need for you to be viewed by the pupils as consistent. Pupils do not like to feel as though they are being picked on. Forget your personal feelings about a student and be consistent with any punishment or reprimand.

On occasion you may well have one of those customary bad days we all experience in teaching. In terms of student behaviour, never 'lose it' with a pupil. It's just not worth it. If you regularly 'lose it' then you will become a figure of humour and held in poor esteem. A Year 8 pupil reflected upon his Science teacher's endless eruptions:

> 'She's always going off her trolley and sometimes goes ballistic for no reason. It's weird. We all think she needs help.'

Poor pupil behaviour, and how you manage it, can often be helped by balancing your language of discipline with words of encouragement. If you have a good working relationship with a class then any misbehaviour from an individual or group should be interpreted as not only their letting you down but also letting themselves down. A classic example from Year 8:

> 'We'd just come in from PE and were high as kites, noisy and loud. Mr Morley sent us all out of the class and made us line up outside again. He said that this was not the sort of behaviour he expected of us and he appeared quite shocked and angry. He's a top bloke and a blinding teacher. I think we all realized we'd upset him. When we came in again we all got down to it.'

Your success as a teacher in the eyes of your pupil

clientele is principally gauged by the way you operate and retain control in the classroom. Skilful management of behaviour creates a positive learning environment. It is a craft that you will hopefully improve with time.

Pupils say that the way teachers treat them as individuals has a major bearing on the learning process. They want you, as the teacher, to understand that they are all different. Some are confident, some timid, some extremely sensitive and some as bold as a Trojan warrior. One of the things they find most irritating is when a teacher fails to learn the names of members in their teaching group. Students prefer you to use their first name when you address them rather than the prehistoric practice of using their surname. Pupils do not want you to patronize them. They want you to treat them as responsible people. However, they do understand that your patience will, at times, be tested to extremes by some characters and you do have their sympathy. One Year 11 girl made the observation:

> 'The frequent immature antics of some of the boys in my group must make it difficult for our teacher to treat us all as responsible young adults.'

Above all, they will find it possible to connect with you if you can still remember what it was like to be a teenager. It is all about creating a climate of mutual respect. They say it's showing you are human and not some automaton insensitive to differences in age and feelings. Another Year 11 pupil commented:

> 'Miss has a good way with our group. She values our opinions. She is human. She's completely the opposite to Mr Prothero, who makes us feel like cattle on a ranch. We all look forward to her lessons.'

When you take on a new teaching class, being perceived as too friendly is a cardinal sin in anyone's book. This error of judgement is often perpetrated by teachers new to the job. Pupils will expect you to be approachable and easy to talk to but being too matey is not good for you or the troops. Your discipline with the group will soon suffer and pupils will start to take liberties. They also don't want you to be too trendy or permissive. Despite the climate of openness and mutual respect you are trying to create, they do expect from you certain standards and control. Some teachers are perceived by pupils as too flash. One young PE member of staff would frequently be seen leaving the school in his wide bore exhaust Subaru revving his engine as he passed girls from Year 13. An articulate Year 12 referred to him as the quintessential Essex Rude Boy. The chap was a source of amusement and commanded little respect.

I also heard of one young male teacher who would be driven to school by his girlfriend and they would be seen passionately embracing before they both parted, each for a morning's work. One aspiring medic of Year 11, who was quite shocked at their antics, reported to his tutor:

> 'I mean, I've heard of tongues, Miss, but this was endoscopy.'

One major cause of breakdown in relationships between pupils and teachers is when teachers fail to provide them with positive and constructive feedback on the quality of their work. It is essential to remember that the work we have set and logged in our planners has been completed by the motley crew sat in front of us and they have done what has been asked of them. Nothing is more disheartening for pupils than spending considerable time on a piece of work and having their books returned to them unmarked. I am sure that because of the pressure of work and when the unexpected arises, we have all been guilty of this at some time. However, this will be acceptable to pupils if it's a 'one-off'. It is completely demotivating if this occurs frequently and also sours any hope of pupil–teacher bonhomie.

Perhaps the most insulting and hurtful thing you can do to a pupil is to lose their coursework. Indeed, such an act is both negligent and unprofessional. I worked with a colleague whose office was like the Bermuda Triangle where coursework was concerned. His lack of organization and amnesia precipitated the following agonizing remarks from one pupil:

> 'I spent over 60 hours on this GCSE coursework. Not only has he not marked it, he now says he can't find it. I'm really worried about my GCSE grade.'

Another disgruntled fellow from Key Stage 4 pleaded his case:

> 'He's had those tests we did for three weeks now and not returned them. We call him Mr Mañana.'

You should never betray a student's trust in you, either as their teacher or as a professional. In my view it is a serious disciplinary matter.

Pupils do appreciate recognition for their efforts. They do welcome suggestions on ways by which they can improve pieces of work. This feedback should be positive and not appear as an overdose of red biro. If the work needs detailed surgery then it should not be undertaken publicly but on a 'one-to-one'. A member of Year 7 moaned:

> 'I spent two hours on that diagram and answering that question and all I got was a tick!'

Kids like celebrating their achievement. They get off on praise and relish it even more if their good work and efforts are made public. It's all part of creating an environment for learning. The use of displays of student work will certainly reward achievement and give a sense of ownership. However, watch out for:

> 'I tried hard with that piece of work and she never put it up on the wall.'
> 'Those displays have been on the wall for ages. My brother who's married now with a kid says they were there when he was at school.'

I do have tremendous sympathy for those teachers who do not have their own permanent teaching bases. Some poor souls wander the schools like commercial travellers and have nowhere to display their wares.

In our quest to treat our students as individuals and to remain alert about their feelings and motivation, we must remember that kids respond well to verbal praise and encouragement. As one Year 7 observed:

> 'Miss said she was dead pleased when I done that bit of writing. It made me feel good.'

A Year 8 pupil appeared quite reborn in terms of drive and enthusiasm when his Maths teacher shook his hand and said:

> 'Delroy, what a terrific piece of work. I'm recommending you for the Nobel Prize for Maths.'
>
> 'Thanks, Sir, but any chance of the money instead?' replied an elated Delroy.

It can be easy to unintentionally hurt a pupil in the way you are seen to respond to their answers to your questions. You should try to leave them with a positive, even when their answer is completely off-target. A question such as

> 'Can anyone tell me what we mean by asexual reproduction?'

may produce the inoffensive and well-meaning answer

> 'Is it when an animal does it to himself?'

Your response to this priceless riposte should not be to roll around on the floor in hysterics in a similar way to the rest of the class. Your professional feedback should include praise and recognition of their efforts and a suggestion that their reply was almost accurate. You will hear some corking theory from your pupils throughout your teaching career, and it's these, often innocent answers that will keep you young. Never put down students in the way you respond to their answers – you will destroy their motivation and lower their self-esteem and eagerness to participate if you do.

A summary of what the pupils say

1 We prefer YOU to be in control in the classroom rather than us.

2. We like you to be firm but fair.
3. We don't like it if you pick on certain people.
4. We like to be clear about what you expect from us when you first teach us and not to find out as we go through the year.
5. We like you to be consistent with rewards and punishments.
6. We like to know you are human.
7. We often find a teacher's irrational mood swings difficult to accept.
8. We like to be treated as individuals if there is to be a feeling of mutual respect.
9. We don't like you to be trendy or permissive.
10. We want you to mark our work and give us feedback on how we are doing.
11. Please don't keep us waiting for test results or marked work.
12. If we ever give a wrong answer to one of your questions then please don't show us up in front of our classmates.
13. We don't mind criticism as long as it's constructive.
14. We respond well to encouragement and your telling us we have done well.
15. We like you to display our work. It gives us a good feeling about ourselves.

3 Teaching and learning (2)

Lena Youssouf was undisputedly 'femme savant'. This wise lady was almost the complete teacher. It was disappointing for her teaching colleagues and for the pupils she taught that she was bereft of a sense of humour. Nowhere on her chromosomes could geneticists map a gene for seeing the funny side of things. As part of a school self-evaluation programme I observed one of her Year 10 lessons. She was faultless in terms of her subject knowledge, pace and challenge of her lesson. Her theme was to do with the richness of biodiversity in the world (lots of different animals and plants, for colleagues who think David Attenborough's *Planet Earth* is a trendy restaurant in London's West End).

She mentioned the fact that the smallest fish in the world had recently been discovered in a lake somewhere in Queensland, Australia. One member of the group raised his hands and offered the information:

> 'The smallest fish, Miss? You ought to go to Wong's Chippy. My Dad reckons they serve the smallest fish in the world, Miss.'

His classmates roared with laughter. I too was glad I was not drinking something at the time. Poor Lena, though, could not quite share the witticism and gave the truthful reply:

> 'I'm sorry, Dean, I don't understand.'

Having a sense of humour is, to a teacher, what a passport must be to Michael Palin. It is a prerequisite for the job. Humour, used properly, can be a powerful and constructive addition to any lesson. There is, however, a clear distinction between humour and sarcasm. There may be a time and place in your personal repertoire for sarcasm but this should never be employed in your dealings with youngsters. They do not respond well to such mockery and see it as an instrument for conveying contempt. Similarly, there is no case for humiliating a student or being overcritical. Some teachers use this technique as put-downs. Pupils find such a practice both hurtful and degrading. One Year 8 told me:

> 'I hate his lessons. He says some really unkind things to us. He thinks he's being funny.'

Another recipient of ridicule from Year 11 stated:

> 'She uses sarcasm as a way of trying to control us. She says some spiteful things.'

Disparaging remarks from teachers do not help:

> 'I don't look forward to teaching you lot. You are a blot on my week.'

You may think such things and even confide with your colleagues of your negativity but in no way should you articulate such pessimism to members of your teaching group.

One of the first things kids say about teachers is that you should know what they are talking about. Whether it's giving advice or putting across information on a teaching subject, to use the vernacular, they expect you to know your arse from your elbow. This is particularly important if you teach human biology. They require you to possess in-depth knowledge about the topic you are sharing with them. They then feel confident to discuss or explore the subject material with you. Coupled with this fundamental premise, they expect you to be able to deliver your knowledge in such a way that they can understand what you are talking about. One young recipient of a raw deal explained:

> 'He may have more degrees than a thermometer and a Ph.D in Geography but he certainly can't teach it!'

Kids lose confidence, feel insecure and eventually see through you if you are not in command of your subject. They lose respect for you. Despite the fact that pupils appreciate your honesty about apparent gaps in your knowledge, their patience and understanding soon wear thin when they feel they are not making progress and grasping the subject. An aspiring Year 10 physicist had concerns when her new GCSE Physics teacher (a biologist by trade) kept on using the unit of watts when talking about energy.

> 'Don't you mean joules, Sir?' she enquired.
>
> 'Er, erm, erm, joules?' muttered Sir Isaac Newton, desperately trying to remember what he'd read last evening.
>
> 'The unit of power is watts, isn't it, Sir?' continued the girl.

Then, realizing that for the past 15 minutes he had, in fact, been shooting himself in the foot and guilty of imparting dubious information, he replied:

> 'Oh, did I say watts, Nicola? Slip of the tongue. Easily done. Sorry!'

Not good for your classroom cred.

Teachers who read from textbooks because of their dilute subject knowledge (yes, it still happens) will also quickly disengage the students. Situations like this can happen when someone teaches out of their subject specialism. Their crowded timetable gives them insufficient time to prepare. I recall one desperate Head teacher, having scrutinized my O levels, asking me if I wouldn't mind teaching French to a Year 7 class for a month or so while a gentleman from French Equatorial Africa, as it was then, got his visa sorted out.

If you are not on top of your subject then you do not give good value for money, and remember, we are dealing with kids' futures. One A level student pondered:

> 'I know he's the Deputy Head but that's no excuse for him failing to turn up to our lessons. Explanations like "Something urgent has cropped up" wear a bit thin after a while. I need his input to get me a strong grade to study Pharmacology at uni.'

'It's the way I tell 'em!' is Frank Carson's catchphrase. Having sound subject knowledge is essential but the way you impart such information is a skill teachers are supposed to hone throughout their career. Mr Carson is right. It's the quality of the delivery of your lesson plan that leads to successful learning. Youngsters want you to pitch information at the right level. Transfer of information should be in such a way that the lesson is perceived as interesting and easy to understand. Teaching should motivate and maintain such interest. If a teacher takes the time to explain things using appropriate language and vocabulary then they instantly join the 'good teacher' category. The following two observations by Year 9 pupils highlight these judgements:

> 'Maths ain't my subject but I enjoy it a lot more since we had Mr Phillips. He explains things.'

> 'I looked at the topic in the textbook. It looked too hard but everything fell into place when Miss explained it.'

Using the right words to explain something means examining your lexicon. Any new terminology you use should be carefully presented in such a way that your words make sense to pupils. At home you may be the champion of Scrabble but at school you should choose your terms carefully. Clarity of expression is welcomed by students.

You may feel that parts of the syllabus you are required to teach are as dry as the Sahara. Your skill is to dress up this tedious material and present it in such a way that will motivate and inspire. This is often easier said than done but not impossible. You should always try to link what you are teaching with the world outside the classroom and engage your pupils with everyday examples. The following Year 11 girl gave credit to her Chemistry teacher's efforts:

> 'I'm a 15 year old who wants to be a beauty therapist. Chemistry is dead boring but Mr Shaw tries to bring it to life by making us see that chemicals are with us all the time.'

Standing in front of a class for the first time may be your initial brush with public speaking. You should make certain your voice carries to the rear of the room without sounding like Barry Scott of the Cillit Bang advertisement on TV. Students find this shouting quite wearying and say poor voice control does not contribute to the enjoyment of the lesson. Students prefer you to vary the pace of your lessons. You should be mindful too of the calibre of your oratory and the way you link sentences. I once worked opposite a colleague who used the sentence link 'Erm' more times than the word 'love' on a Barry White CD. It can tend to move you into the 'boring' category. Watch out too for your overdosing the group with the expressions 'OK', 'Right' and 'Alright'.

If you ever record one of your lessons on tape then you will find this can often highlight something that is in need of improvement. You may discover you have the most boring monotone voice or an irritating mannerism. The kids have known of this misfortune since you started teaching them but because of the engrained classroom protocol have not been able to discuss this – with you, anyway. One disappointed member of Year 12 was heard to say:

> 'Mr Kerrigan's lessons invariably induce a corporate coma. His voice is unchanging. It lacks pitch, intonation and is void of inspiration. I believe I have found the cause of the disease narcolepsy.'

If you endeavour to provide a variety of stimulating and interesting work for your students then you will be able to create a relaxed and enjoyable learning atmosphere in the classroom. To bring this about it is essential that lessons are carefully planned. It is crucial, therefore, that you are clear in your own mind as to the learning objectives for each lesson. The students too should know what they are expected to achieve by the end of each session. They are, therefore, not allergic to the clear lesson aims and objectives being written on the board and having them explained at the start. We have Ofsted to thank for this, though I am loath to praise this group of assassins for anything. Explicit aims and objectives, then, are a must for all your lessons. In days of yore, I have heard pupils moan:

> 'He didn't tell us what the lesson was all about and what we really had to do.'

Pupils also think it reasonable to see how things they learn today will dovetail and relate to things they have learned before. This will avoid a group member scratching his head and grumbling:

> 'I couldn't follow what he was talking about. It didn't seem to have anything to do with what we done last time.'

They see the relevance of putting into practice the skills and knowledge they have learned from previous lessons. This reinforcement strengthens the learning process. The way you interact with students and groups maintains their enthusiasm and momentum. They prefer you to move among groups and spend time talking to them.

> 'Miss keeps our group work going by chatting to us regular.'

Once you have decided upon what you want to teach and the lesson objectives are clear in your mind, then good planning requires you to think about how you will deliver these objectives.

There is much spoken about the best practices teachers should employ for effective learning to take place. One cynical teacher on the verge of retirement claimed:

> 'If I kept my teaching style constant for thirty years then educationalists would feel my technique would be in vogue at least twice over that period of time.'

I have no problem with this gentleman's prediction as long as his lessons do provide his pupils with a variety of stimulating and interesting work. Pupils do prefer lessons where their teachers can vary their teaching technique and where the teaching clearly supports different learning styles.

Differentiation is often perceived as a panic inducing term among secondary school teachers. Many feel it is a principle for which they lack the necessary rudimentary skills and knowledge. Nevertheless, it is a fundamental educational premise that pupils learn differently and that differentiation underpins personalized learning. Sound, effective classroom teaching is based on the principles of differentiation whether this be by task or by outcome. The former is when the teacher gives the pupils in the class a different task to do. Differentiation by outcome is where all pupils are given the same undertaking but an allowance is made for a range of possible outcomes according to individual capabilities.

Differentiation is successfully practised in primary education. Youngsters coming through the primary–secondary transfer expect this approach to continue. One Year 7 lamented:

> 'A lot of our lessons are different to our last school. We have to do a lot more sitting and listening to the teacher.'

Setting does not completely avoid the practice of differentiation. Establishing more homogeneous groups reduces the spread of ability. However, the teacher must still accept that children learn in different ways and that we should show sensitivity to this principle by planning a suitable range of activities.

If we accept the proposition that differentiation should be the foundation for our classroom practice and a vehicle for improving teaching and learning then whole schools should have an ethos committed to this principle. This allegiance should be reflected in departmental policies, guidelines for lesson plans and target setting processes.

Pupils will tolerate didactic performances by teachers as long as this does not occur every lesson. One Year 9 said of her History teacher:

> 'She talks all the time. It's dead borin'.'

Pupils welcome a variety of teacher led activities. Student centred, experiential and collaborative practices should be included in a teaching repertoire.

Kids claim that any practical work they are able to undertake helps them to remember things. This experiential, hands-on approach reduces boredom, they say. One habitual classroom somnolent remarked:

> 'I like it when she lets us do some practical. The lessons are better and they go quicker.'

Another sleeping partner concluded:

> 'I can remember more when we do something different to just listening. When we do practical it sticks more.'

X-ray the above statements and we learn that lessons become more interesting for the student if they are fully occupied. Collaborative learning can also fully engage pupils. They like working in friendship groups where they are able to exchange ideas and skills. However, the structure of such working groups needs careful consideration to avoid overzealous members becoming world dominant. Group work should involve every member and not just the most articulate and authoritarian. Avoid groups that precipitate statements like:

> 'Dean and Louise don't give the rest of us a chance. Dean takes the piss out of what me and Cheryl say so we don't bother.'

Class discussion work enables pupils to feel they are given a voice and an opportunity to air their ideas. Again, it is important for the teacher to ensure that all of the group is involved and not just the most articulate and vociferous. The pupils prefer student centred work to be as a collective exercise rather than working on their own. One discerning Year 11 girl remarked:

> 'Other people's opinions are not always the same as yours but it's good to hear what they think.'

Pupils prefer lessons to be teacher led so they can really understand the task in hand and indeed, your job as the facilitator is to create a task orientated classroom. They feel you can get them more involved by developing effective questioning techniques. They see this methodology as a way of maintaining their interest and participation in the lesson. As one Year 10 student put it:

> 'If he don't ask us questions about what we are doing then we feel he's not really interested.'

Pupils do prefer to be given a sense of challenge in a particular task you set them. However, it is important that this work is within their capabilities. Your acceptance of the principles of differentiation should give an appropriate level of challenge, often referred to as an optimal challenge. Your expectations of pupils must be realistic and there should be no mismatch between what you anticipate from them and the expectations they have of themselves. Students become disheartened if they perceive the work as being too difficult. One Year 8 commented:

> 'He didn't explain properly what we had to do. It was too hard. Me and my mate started mucking about.'

Another disheartened Year 10 Physicist complained:

> 'The work he set for me was too hard. It was beyond me. I don't catch on to things easy. He should know that by now. He's been teaching us all year.'

Even more perturbing was one comment from a fellow Year 10:

> 'When we do some topic that's really hard and I don't get it, he says I haven't been listening properly and I have.'

Teachers are thus expected to know the group and be cognizant of individual capabilities and potential. Tasks should be sufficiently demanding to give a sense of real learning but not to be too demanding.

The converse of this also applies in that they become frustrated by the work set being too easy. The challenge is not there and they become bored and troublesome. One budding female academic readily confessed:

> 'We did the work, it was dead easy. He gave us 20 minutes to do it and we did it in five. After that we just chatted about Lewis Perry in Year 10. He's gorgeous.'

Some well-intentioned lessons are totally impractical because of time constraints. Looking at your watch and realizing you are in the 'middle' phase of your lesson when the bell is just about to sound is a fundamental error. The perils of such an elementary oversight should have been highlighted on your teacher-training programme. The kids know you've messed up and say things such as:

> 'We won't have time to get all our results, Sir. How are we going to write this up?'

On occasions, the pupils will point out your lack of the concept of time by scoring own goals. A classic example is when you panic and rush the last five minutes of the lesson in an attempt to include all the items in your lesson plan. As the students are hurriedly escaping from the classroom, you suddenly realize you haven't set them any homework and the last one is heard saying:

> 'Ain't we got homework, then, tonight, Miss?'

Your immediate thoughts are:

> 'Blast! That's the second week on the trot I've done that. I really must get better at timing my lessons.'

The thoughts of the kids are:

> 'Great! That's the second week on the trot she's done that. She really should get better at timing her lessons.'

In conclusion, pupils value teachers who clearly show they have injected plenty of effort in the planning of their lessons.

You will sometimes use new equipment and apparatus to enhance the delivery and presentation of your lessons. It is absolutely essential you know exactly how to use these accoutrements, otherwise you will look a banana and your lesson will lose its pace and interest. As you struggle with the interactive whiteboard, which for the past few minutes has proved totally inactive, your command of student enthusiasm and lesson momentum will slowly drift away. The students register their disappointment by cranking up the background noise. Such errors do nothing for your classroom credibility.

Nevertheless, pupils do appreciate the use of this modern technology in their lessons. They say they prefer interactive whiteboards to the use of overhead projectors. They see the latter as old fashioned and dated technology almost akin to the Victorian use of chalk and slate. Some students point out that teachers can use overkill with interactive whiteboards. They feel there are some presentations that would be better delivered without this gadgetry. The effective use of video, DVD and computers are also seen to complement lessons.

I have known some Science teachers order apparatus and chemicals they have never before used. I must emphasize this is a dodgy and downright dangerous prescription for laboratory success. In practical subjects you have to be even more concerned about health and safety matters. If you have just showered half the class with mercury and you hear comments such as

> 'Blimey, Sir! That shouldn't have happened, should it?'

your trust with the class as a knowledgeable scientist will

rapidly wane as well as your receiving questions from the Head teacher, parents and governors about your laboratory proficiency.

Time for assessment based activities needs to be incorporated into your planning. We can monitor student progress by a variety of methods and not just by giving them written end-of-topic tests. Constructive assessment can also be by quiz, informal observation of group work, discussion and problem setting. Such assessment should be used for future planning and involvement. One Year 9, who was clearly pleased with her teacher's approach to assessment, aired her opinions as:

> 'To see how well we have understood our work she gives us crosswords, word searches, filling in blanks and quizzes. Our class likes them. It's not like some of the boring tests we have from some teachers.'

Homework should be seen as a vehicle for building on work that has been done in class. Homework should be something that is built into our lesson plans. Pupils expect homework to be set. They are issued with a homework timetable. Parents too scrutinize student planners and homework diaries. The quality and the nature of homework should be seen to have a purpose. It should tie in and complement the work undertaken in the lesson.

Homework can take on different forms and students welcome such variation. However, some students feel that certain teachers set homework for homework's sake. Pupils easily see through such tokenism and will respond accordingly. In the same way, homework needs to be brought into the same assessment arena as the work pupils do in class. Purposefully set, relevant and regularly assessed homework is an integral part of extending and reinforcing the learning process.

The monitoring and assessment of student progress is a duty we must not sideline in our teaching. Students are often anxious to know how they are doing. This is particularly important when they are preparing for public tests and examinations. If our monitoring and assessment procedures are in place then realistic prognoses can be given to both students and their parents. I did, however, overhear one young male PE teacher being asked about examination potential by one of his GCSE class members:

> 'What sort of grade do you reckon I'll get in PE, Sir?'
>
> 'I never forecast anything, Marvin, and I predict I never will do,'

was the Corinthian's reply. Marvin retreated from the rendezvous confused on two counts.

A summary of what the pupils say

1. We like teachers to have a sense of humour because it shows us you are human.
2. We don't like you to be sarcastic, too critical of us or to belittle what we say.
3. We like teachers to have a sound working knowledge of the subject they teach and to be able to answer our questions truthfully.
4. If you don't know the answer to something then be honest and don't feed us bulls**t.
5. Try to liven up the delivery and pace of your lessons. Please don't be boring even though the topic may want you to think of suicide.

6 We like you to explain things to us. You may pick things up quickly but some of us don't.
7 We like you to use language we understand when you explain something.
8 We like teachers who clearly show us they have put a real effort into preparing the lesson.
9 We like lessons to have a clear point to them.
10 We like the aims and objectives of the lesson to be put on the board at the start of the lesson.
11 We like you to understand that we learn in different ways and at different paces.
12 We like to experience a range of activities and for you to vary the way you teach.
13 We like you to lead the lesson and give us clear directions.
14 We like to be given practical work or work in groups.
15 We also don't mind class discussion so that we can see other people's points of view.
16 We like you to move around the classroom and talk to us about our work.
17 We want you to ask us questions in the lesson about what we think or what we have learned.
18 We like lessons to have some challenge but not so hard that we cannot do it. We like you to have a realistic understanding of what we can do and achieve.
19 We like to be able to put into practice the new things we have learned.
20 We like to see how things we have learned before fit in with the things we are learning now.
21 We know you have to see how well we have learned something but we like you to test us in different ways.
22 We expect homework but it should be relevant to the work we have done or are about to do. We like different sorts of homework.

23 We like you to use interactive whiteboards and other learning gadgets but don't use them for using's sake.
24 We don't mind your asking us if you are not sure about how a computer works.

4 Form tutors

'Ours don't do nuffink.'

This was the curt, yet honest analysis of Mr Wolstenholme's participation as Loretta Blanchette's form tutor. I overheard such syntactical inaccuracy when I was doing a cover lesson. A young lady seated opposite the sonorous Loretta was in the process of outlining the virtues and commitment of Mrs Saville, another tutor, to her flock. Edna Saville was an asset to any pastoral team. She demonstrated all the personal and professional qualities needed for successful form tutoring. She could transfer and apply these skills to any year group.

It is regrettable that form tutoring for some teachers is seen as a bolt-on exercise and a burdensome teaching duty. Cynicism of this nature propagates a reluctance to participate. Those who see tutoring as a chore fail to accept that when they sign up to join the teaching army it is expected that you give allegiance to the whole job package. Your capacity as form tutor to a group of 26 youngsters not only plays a responsible role but is also a productive and worthwhile commission.

In education today we seem to be obsessed with the word 'learning'. Year Heads are referred to as Learning Managers, pupils are Learners, PE staff promote the principles of Fitness for Learning and no doubt we will soon be appointing caretaking staff with the grand title of Curators for Learning.

I felt a sense of disappointment when I heard a member of staff introduce himself to a tutor group as their Learning Tutor. To a degree, I can understand Ofsted's obsessive rationale that underpins such labelling. Indeed, a happy and contented child has more chance of succeeding as an effective learner than one who continues to experience problems in their developing years. To kids, the title Learning Tutor tends to remove the personal dimension of form tutoring and to focus solely on academic achievement. Therefore, I prefer the title Personal Tutor, one that encompasses concern for the child both as an individual and as a student.

Tutors who are seen to readily connect with their tutees and get the best out of them seem to display similar qualities and characteristics.

> 'He's alright, Mr Armison, you can talk to him.'

This type of statement about a tutor is a common response when students are asked 'What do you think makes a good tutor?' The fact that you as a tutor are seen to be approachable and someone with whom pupils can have comfortable dialogue has significant meaning to them. Many pupils find difficulty in talking openly and honestly to their parents.

> 'I can't talk to my Mum, she's always moaning. Me Dad's never in.'

Pupils welcome an opportunity to talk with adults and seek their opinions. The tutor may be asked to fulfil this role particularly when there are issues at home. You may be able to offer a solution to a problem or suggest ways of communicating this difficulty to the parents. Youngsters will speak with you about many things if they feel they can trust you.

> 'I asked Mr Whelan what he thinks. He's a geezer.'

Tutors see the students in their charge on average twice a day. In short, they have far more contact with their tutees than any other teacher in the school and hence are expected to have the most knowledge of these people. You can only possess this information if you talk to them.

> 'Miss talks with us, not at us.'

Young people will connect with you more if you let them know you remember what it's like to be a teenager. If there is a mutual respect then they will open up to you. They may wish to ask your views on a subject. They may have a problem with a certain subject or teacher. There may be issues with friends. Other than their mates, you may be the only alternative and the only person with whom they feel they can speak. Being a good listener is an essential skill.

I worked with a young tutor who was highly rated by her group. She too gave them her time after completing the daily minutiae. I recall part of a conversation she had with a talented Year 10 footballer. The tutor was concerned that the lad was tempted to forfeit his GCSEs for the sake of a professional football apprenticeship. The tutor asked:

> 'How far do you want to go in football, Vassos?'
>
> 'Well, I'd like to go to China, Miss,'

was the pensive reply. It's all in a day's work, I suppose.

If it's difficult to speak at length with one of your group at that point in time then always create space for them during that day. The matter may be trivial or a potentially serious one. Make time for them, that's the important thing.

The nature of what a pupil will disclose to you can be anything from girl/boyfriend trouble to family breakdown. Often it's something as benign as not getting into a certain team or a problem with a particular homework. The thing to remember is that the subject matter is important to them and that they value your counsel.

> 'My mate moved house to Birmingham last week and I felt really down. Mrs Walters noticed I looked fed up and we chatted about it. She cheered me up.'

Certain disclosures will force you to remember your professional boundaries. Serious domestic problems or those that touch on child protection issues will force you to enlist the help of outside support and intervention bodies. Some youngsters may not want this to happen. Nevertheless, you have a professional duty, relating to the school's child protection policy, to inform the youngster that you cannot keep such a weighty affair to yourself. You act as a catalyst in the help process.

> 'My tutor just seemed the right person to talk to when my Dad started knocking my Mother about. We like her 'cos she's easy to talk to. And she seems to care about us. I spoke to a friend and she came with me. It was because of her that the school got Social Services involved. Something had to be done for my Mum's sake.'

One fairly rapid lesson you learn as a tutor is you have to develop mediation skills. You may be asked to liaise with teaching colleagues about matters relating to homework, assessment, discipline or even the way they deliver their lessons.

> 'Mrs Carrison gives us tons of homework, so much that we can't do the other stuff we are set. We complained to Mr Dennis, our tutor, and he said he'd see what he could do.'

You will also feel it necessary to liaise with other pupils about disagreements or actions that are causing the unhappiness of one of your tutees. It may be with parents that you feel your duty is to act as arbitrator over contentious issues.

> 'My Mum and Dad expected me to do three hours of revision a night for my GCSEs. This was from Christmas onwards. My tutor rang them up and arranged a meeting to explain how much work I should be doing. It helped. We reached a compromise as my tutor called it but they're still mental about school things.'

Certain tutors who feel uncomfortable with the tutor role are reluctant to shoulder disciplinary issues relating to their tutees. They feel such punitive action should be the responsibility of the classroom teacher, Head of Department or Head of Year. We all have a collective responsibility for discipline and upholding acceptable standards of behaviour in a school. As a form tutor you have an immediate undertaking to maintain such high standards. The relationship you forge with them will complement your disciplinary role. You should strive to establish a relationship that if students let themselves down because of poor behaviour then they also will disappoint and upset you. If you appear insincere or carefree about them then they will feel the same way about you.

> 'I let off some fart gas spray in the corridor and the caretaker reported me to the Head. Miss Tarpey told me she'd

> also been seen by the Head, who gave her a bad time too. I felt rotten about that, 'cos she's OK.'

The members of your group expect you to uphold the school rules and set high standards.

In school uniform matters, again, it's down to you. You see pupils at the start of school and you should expect their cooperation in being suitably attired. Good control means you only have to look at them and they know they are incorrectly dressed.

> 'Yes, Sir, I'm putting 'em on.'

This reply concerned itself with trainers and not trousers. If you don't pick them up on fundamental issues such as uniform then they sense you are not doing a tutor's job.

The school calendar will insist upon your tutor group becoming involved in activities such as sports day, the inter-tutor group or house competitions as well as year assemblies. You are more likely to experience success at organizing the participation of your group if you have a positive relationship with them. If you have created a sense of identity and a feeling of *esprit de corps* among your group members then you are more likely to field a full squad, each player not wanting to let the side down. The way you are with the kids determines their loyalty.

> 'Nobody else really wanted to do the 1500 metres. Our tutor looked at me with a smile 'cos I hadn't volunteered for anything. "Go on, then," I said, "I'll do it." Only 'cos he's well good with us.'

If you seem apathetic about your tutor role then this indifference will transfer to the kids. Your group assemblies and the extra-curricular commitments of your group will suffer. To create a sense of belonging and corporate spirit you should try to involve the students as much as possible. Give them individual responsibilities. I recall a friend and teaching colleague allocating each pupil a specific responsibility within his tutor group with amazing results. Subsequently, the likes of Bodrul Patel and Phillipa Tattersall, who were known for having as much energy as a moribund slug, came out of their comatose states and tackled their duties as Chief Ventilation Engineer and Notice Board Consultant with gusto. The kids loved it.

TUTOR GROUP 8W RESPONSIBILITIES

Title of Position of Responsibility	Person
Form Captain: Male	Damon Wallace
Form Captain: Female	Nicole Windlas
Health and Safety Officer 1	Zak Martinez
Health and Safety Officer 2	Delores Golding
Information Distribution Officer 1	Mesut Zamrutel
Information Distribution Officer 2	Charmaine Fink
Register Executive 1	Dion Felix
Register Executive 2	Carlos St Jean
Appraisal Manager 1	Dean Deane
Appraisal Manager 2	Troy Mergolees
Chief Ventilation Engineer 1	Bodrul Patel
Chief Ventilation Engineer 2	Kami Tailor
Notice Board Consultant 1	Phillipa Tattersall
Notice Board Consultant 2	Edson Quigley
Advertising Supremo 1	Ellice Dupres
Advertising Supremo 2	James Patterson
Classroom Manager	Zuleema Horsewell
Sports Captain: Male	Theo Oluwayu
Sports Captain: Female	Emma Crosby
Homework Coordinator 1	Otis Farrell
Homework Coordinator 2	Ranjeet Singh
School Council Representative 1	Mike Walling
School Council Representative 2	Maisie Bent
Classroom Maintenance Engineer 1	Panay Andreou
Classroom Maintenance Engineer 2	Naomi Bradley

It tends to spook kids if their tutor is too serious all the time. If they call you human then they will expect you to have a sense of humour. Some of the things your tutees will say and do will make you laugh and if you can reciprocate then so much the better. I recall a middle-aged tutor for whom I had the greatest respect entering her tutor room only to find one of her Year 10 boys dancing around while listening to his iPod.

> 'Erm, put the iPod away, please, Luke!' requested the tutor.
>
> 'Oh, yes, sorry, Miss,' replied Luke, peeling the cables from his ears. 'Do you like hip hop, Miss?' he enquired, still bobbing up and down.
>
> 'Do I like hip 'op, Luke? Hip 'op? I'm bloomin' well having one next term!'

The class dissolved with laughter.

You are the first point of contact for parents. This may be as simple as their telephoning the school to explain an absence. It may, however, be a more detailed communication concerning the progress of their son or daughter. It could also be information that could have bearings on their child's happiness or welfare. Domestic problems may deserve an explanation.

> 'When my Dad left, my Mum contacted Mr Lomax, my tutor, to put him in the picture. He said he'd only tell my teachers if my Mum and me both wanted them to know. He had a word with me at lunchtime and was very kind.'
>
> 'My Dad rang my tutor because I was getting a real thing about Chemistry. I couldn't understand it and Mr Quinn was not the kind of teacher who explains things properly.
>
> My tutor said she'd see what help she could be. Nothing happened so he rang her again. She apologized and said

> she'd forgotten but would see him today. That was two weeks ago. She's a waste of time so he's rung my Head of Year.'

The kids should rely upon you and trust you. If you say you are going to do something then make sure you do it. We all are busy people but when there is a cry for help from a tutee, be there for them. There may be special circumstances where you must play a part even though you may feel ill at ease with your role. Some tutors who have never experienced serious family problems themselves may feel out of their depth or uncomfortable discussing such issues with a parent or child. Sickness at home, a family bereavement, separation and divorce are circumstances that you may face relating to pupils in your charge. It's knowing what to say and do that tests your capacity for tutoring.

> 'My Gran's moved in with us 'cos she's not well. Trouble is, she's in my room and I've had to move in with me brother. My tutor, Mrs Appleby, has made arrangements for me to stay after school to do my homework in her tutor room. I can't do it in me brother's room, it's too noisy.'

> 'When me Mam cleared off, me Dad rang me tutor to tell him. All he did was smile at me more. I don't think he knew what to say to me.'

When a pupil loses someone close to them it can throw to the surface all kinds of feelings. Grief can precipitate many emotional changes. There may be a sense of emptiness, numbness, anger or guilt. Some tutors feel they are out of their depth in dealing with bereavement. As a tutor you cannot ignore the responsibility you have to a child in your group who loses a parent, sibling, grandparent or close friend.

> 'Mrs Ball was kind when my Gran died. She said she knew exactly how I was feeling 'cos she was really close to her Nan and we talked about how I miss her.'
>
> 'Mr Delaney just kept saying how sorry he was when my little brother died. I really wanted to talk about it but I could tell he seemed not to know what to say.'

Should you feel uncomfortable or lacking in experience about the way you as a tutor should respond to such challenging circumstances then seek help. Your Head of Year should be there for you and offer some constructive advice. If you have never written a letter of condolence before then they should help you.

> 'I got a letter from Mrs Lawson, my tutor. It was a nice and kind letter saying how sorry she was about me losing my Dad. She said that the school will give me all the support I may need and how sad my friends in the tutor group were. She came to the funeral with two of my best friends. My Mum rang to thank her for her letter and to chat about a few things.'

There are many things in teaching for which we pay homage to computers, in the way they make our administrative chores easier. However, there is one duty, namely the recording of a presence or an absence of a pupil, that can be made more complex and bewildering by their service. Back in time, a presence was when a bum was on a seat and an absence was when this bum was not on its seat. Thanks to electronic intervention there are now approximately nine ways of saying someone is not there in your group. Many tutors still cannot get to grips with what constitutes authorized and unauthorized absences. Often letters of enquiry are sent home unnecessarily only to receive a terse reply from an offended parent. It's all about you as a tutor being in control and some feel that electronic registry can work against your organized system.

> 'On my report it had me down for two unauthorized absences. I gave a letter to my tutor both times when I had to go to the orthodontist. My Mum went mad at me and thought I was bunkin' off.'

Make certain you read absence notes, date them and have them filed. Check for their authenticity. The school should have a mechanism in place for dealing with first day calling and disseminating absence information received by administrative staff to tutors. Do not assume that kids whose behaviour is akin to Mother Teresa's may never be tempted go AWOL on the odd occasion. I am mindful of a currently successful world class snooker player whose previous school attendance record was undisputedly 100 per cent. The young man in my group suddenly started absenting himself in Year 11 for occasional days. He was, in fact, systematically annihilating middle aged snooker title-holders at the local hall and doing so playing in his school blazer.

Kids expect you to be organized in terms of registration procedures and if you are not they will take advantage of this weakness.

> 'Miss Gilbert don't know what planet she's on. We can tell her anything and she swallows it.'

The antithesis of the above opinion was once told to me:

> 'He's sharp, Sir. He don't let anything get past him, even Jasmine O'Grady don't try skiving off any more.'

Most tutors feel more comfortable with their role as a Learning Tutor. The form tutor is in the unique position to provide support for the processes of student review, reflection and target setting. Tutors should have sufficient time allocated to them to assist with a review and analysis of the achievement of their tutees. ARDs (Academic Review Days) and ASTs (Academic and Social Targeting Days) now provide this forum. It is important, however, that during such consultation sessions you, the pupil or their parents do not overdose on data. Easy to evaluate targets that conform to the SMART (specific, measurable, achievable, relevant and time related) criteria should be established. This avoids the empty prehistoric clichés:

> 'He told me I could do better if I made good progress.'
>
> 'She said I should spend more time revising.'

If we build in the SMART formula then we hear pupils saying:

> 'I have to bring my PE kit to all of my PE lessons for the rest of this term.'

That's the theory, anyway. In any case, target setting is only purposeful and effective if there is follow up. Pupils readily see the exercise as being pointless if nobody is prepared to monitor these goals. One pragmatic Year 9 pointed out:

> 'I went along with this getting me organized lark but he didn't check up on me. So I can't be arsed.'

Many pupils will look to their tutors for help with study skills. Many students openly say they do not know how to revise. They will need help in preparing for tests and public examinations. Revision timetables and revision techniques will be Swahili to some of your tutor flock.

> 'I'm crap at exams but I did get a bit better when our tutor spent some time talking about making things stick. I can't sit there for hours so I like the idea of revising in short bursts.'

Pupils will also check that you are monitoring their homework. Student planners and homework diaries will need checking on a regular basis. It is part of your job description and the pupils expect this duty from you.

> 'Our tutor only looks busy when the Head of Year comes round. Rest of the time he marks books and we saw him do his lottery numbers.'

> 'Our tutor never forgets to check our planners. She shouts out, "Have your passports ready, please, ladies and gentlemen!" '

At some stage in your contact with your tutees you should take an active role in assisting them with the major decisions they will have to make. The grand term is 'planning for the future'. This may be in highlighting strengths and weaknesses as they prepare to hop from Key Stage 3 to 4. Option choices need to be well thought out and pupils will value your interest and advice. They will often seek your opinions on post-16 decisions. It is the relationship you have forged with the group that determines the degree to which they will ask for help.

> 'I'd never really thought about going into nursing. My tutor had told me about his brother being a nurse. He said I would make a good nurse because of the way I am with

> people. He set up an interview with our student services teacher so I could find out more about what qualifications you have to have.'

> 'My tutor says going to college will be better for me than staying on into the sixth form. He says I should take one of those vacational courses.'

One final concern expressed by kids concerns reports. They prefer the tutor to summarize the advice and guidance in the report sheets. They also like the tutor to say something about them as individuals. In other words, they see the tutor report as an analysis of their academic, personal and social development. The majority, however, deplore the use of statement banks. As one none-too-cerebral young man pointed out to me:

> 'My report read as though it had been written by a robot.'

A perspicacious Year 11 lady also added her two ha'p'orth:

> 'Computer generated reports tend to depersonalize everything. I expected unique and sincere comments from my teachers, some of whom have known me for over three years. Instead, I got uninspiring and impersonal messages produced for the mass market.'

Ironically the girl in question went on to be Head Prefect, read English at Oxford and is now an advertising executive who promotes products for the mass market.

A summary of what the pupils say

1. We prefer a tutor who shows an interest in us as people.
2. We like you to be approachable and easy to talk to.
3. We would like to be able to talk with you about all sorts of things and not just school things.
4. We like you to listen to us.
5. We like you to talk with us and not always at us.
6. Sometimes we would like to feel comfortable about asking your opinion as an adult about important things and not just talk to our mates.
7. We may need you to mediate with our parents.
8. We would like to think of you as someone at school who is there for us if we have problems or are in trouble.
9. We accept and understand that you have routine jobs to do such as checking uniform, homework and upholding school standards of discipline.
10. We like you to have a sense of humour.
11. We like you to be firm but fair.
12. We like to be able to trust and depend on you.
13. We like you to get involved in target setting because you know us best.
14. We are likely to be together as a group for a long time and we would like there to be a sense of identity and belonging in the tutor group.
15. We do like to be involved in competition with other tutor groups.
16. We like there to be a mutual respect and for you to treat us as individuals.

5 Middle leaders

A school may have a Head teacher with more vision than a clairvoyant and more goals than Jimmy Greaves but any school improvement programme will become quiescent without its middle leaders signing the pledge. Middle leaders constitute the powerhouse or engine room of any school. It is their work rate that determines the success of this establishment. Head teachers depend upon middle leaders to play a crucial role in promoting the broader strategic vision for school improvement and for monitoring its implementation.

It is unfortunate, however, that some school personnel who carry this title see themselves as middle managers and subject administrators and not as leaders. They see their immediate role as looking after human and teaching resources. The leadership dimension implies knowing what goes on in your subject teaching rooms and providing a mechanism for improving classroom practice. Such monitoring will identify the needs of members of your team and be able to offer them guidance and professional development. Strong leadership enables your team to improve teaching and learning.

Your effectiveness as a middle leader will be determined not only by the way your teaching and support team develops but also by the way the pupils who pursue your curriculum area respond. Strong departmental leaders see a rise in student performance in their subject and an increase in their enthusiasm and participation. Pupils will be able to identify strong and talented subject leaders. If the response of a Year 11 student to the question

> 'Who is the Head of Maths?'

is

> 'I dunno.'

then I would suggest this anonymity falls short of the leadership category.

The monitoring of classroom practice is an essential duty and skill of any departmental leader. This task enables you to take an accurate reading of the temperature of your department and gauge how the pupils are performing in the subject for which you are responsible.

> 'Mrs Rollinson can't control us.'

This is a statement and, indeed, a plea for help that all subject leaders will hear from pupils. It is, therefore, the job of this Head of Department to do something about this and improve the classroom experience for both parties. It may be your lack of leadership that has precipitated the situation. Is there a clear strategy for promoting positive behaviour of students within your subject realm?

> 'Miss spells it out at the beginning of the year to us about how we should behave in a lab. She asks us about what we think about these "standards", as she calls them. We usually agree with her and think they're OK and right.'

> 'Mr Jackson, the Head of English, comes round to our teaching group and sits in the lesson and helps out. I think

> it's because our teacher is too young and finds us a handful.'
>
> 'I used to find his lessons boring when he first came to the school 'cos he was always shouting at us. He's got better at controlling us now and the lessons are better.'

Successful departments are usually mutually supportive. Problems with poor behaviour of students need to be addressed with staff, not only on a one-to-one basis but also by discussing student behaviour as a department. It is a fatal mistake for curriculum heads to simply 'fire-fight' in issues concerning poor behaviour. There needs to be a proactive approach to this problem. There should be colleague support on bad behaviour in lessons. Teachers with sixth form classes or those with small trouble-free groups need to be enlisted for support at crisis times. Their assistance for absorbing a recalcitrant needs careful negotiation and planning. Departmental policy should be clear and consistent on 'time out', sending to or for the Head of Department as well as outlining proper use of the 'senior staff on call' resource.

> 'He sent me out to Harvey, Head of History. Don't know why, he couldn't do much with our class when he had us.'

The above response will not give your team members much hope. They will look to you for direction, assistance and advice about dealing with unacceptable behaviour.

Poor behaviour is accompanied by low expectations. As curriculum leader, it is incumbent upon you to tackle these issues. Are schemes of work of a standard to match the abilities of students within the teaching groups and are they linked with learning outcomes? When was the last time you revisited these schemes of work and do they include suitable enrichment material for the able, gifted and talented? Is there work available for those with specific learning difficulties? Are pupils at all levels of ability suitably engaged? Your job is to make the subject as appealing as possible even within the corset of National Curriculum. How much students enjoy their learning at Key Stage 3 in your subject will impact upon whether they choose this at Key Stage 4. If you manage a core subject then its appeal will gear the way pupils will relish participation at examination level.

> 'Food technology with Mrs Barwick was unbearable in Year 9. My friend's group had Miss Peters and they did lots of interesting things. All we did was theory so I certainly didn't want to opt for it in Year 10.'

You are a catalyst for a team of teachers and they look to you for clarity about their job descriptions, their role and expectations. They will want to see you as organized, giving clear direction and being inspirational. You are no use to any body of staff if your nickname within the faculty is 'www.lastminute.com' or 'Mr Amnesia'.

One Year 10 girl said in praise of one Head of Department:

> 'The Head of PE sends out a newsletter which tells us about things that have happened in the department. It tells us and our parents about things they would not normally get to hear about. My Mum called it a go-ahead department. She's a teacher as well.'

Target setting and monitoring the progress of students against these targets is an area which will demand much of your time. The use of short-term targets should serve to motivate and measure the success of pupils. Subject leaders should spearhead this process and should oversee its implementation. You should not hear:

> 'I'm still not clear about what my targets for this term are. He mentioned about five things and I can only remember one.'

Instead, you know things are going in the direction you want when the response is:

> 'My teacher bigged me up about my work. He said that I could get even better if we worked together on some things maybe a bit at a time. He's given me a target book and we cross 'em off as I do 'em.'

As a Department Manager you will take in exercise books and pieces of work to oversee student progress. It is wise that you pick up on anything the teacher has overlooked and in a tactful way bring it to their attention. Marking should be in accordance with school or departmental policy and completed soon after the work has been set. In tandem with this exercise, ensure that you are happy with how this work has been assessed and that feedback has been given to students. This essential feedback not only allows them to understand how they have done but also shows them how to move forward. The craft of meticulous record keeping starts and ends with you.

> 'My Mum went to see Mrs Davey about the Maths set I'm in. She had all my Maths records there which showed I was in the right group. I told her I was all along but she's always like that.'

You may have a fossil in your department who marks books and teaches in a way you would have found popular in the Pleistocene era. Your vision, the collegiate way you operate with staff and your wish to broaden their experience should help in their pedagogical evolution. If it fails then wait for natural selection.

> 'Mr Garwood is teaching us different to other groups in my year.'

This statement either fills your heart with optimism that he has at last discovered the principles of accelerated learning or, alas, that maybe he is teaching them from the wrong syllabus again this year.

Many Heads of Department are fortunate enough to have a suite of classrooms or a teaching block. It is the responsibility of this subject leader to organize display areas where the good work done in lessons or in departmental clubs or school visits can be displayed and openly celebrated.

Some older and less technologically minded staff are still rather allergic to using IT (Information Technology) in their lessons. Again, it is your persuasive powers and encouragement that will steer them through this gigabyte baptism and hopefully render them match fit for classroom participation. It is anticipated that they will appreciate how other advances in IT can support and improve teaching and learning. A sagacious Year 10 girl once told me:

> 'He's a brilliant teacher, Mr Hardcastle. He really knows his stuff. We did, however, spend a couple of lessons teaching him about the use of spreadsheets. He seems to be making good progress.'

The monitoring of homework set by members of your team is yet another essential duty of middle leaders. Your departmental handbook and the schemes of work should set out details about the use of homework. It is your professional duty to ensure that homework is being set and assessed. There is nothing worse than when a tutor, Head of Year or parent points out to you that this is clearly not happening. You end up with egg, of Humpty Dumpty proportions, on your face. It is a humiliating experience and tends to suggest that you as curriculum leader do not know what is happening within your department.

> 'My Dad rang the Head to tell him that Miss Duffy had not set us any geography homework for the last month. I told him not to phone the Head and that he should contact my tutor but you can't tell him anything.'

Such exposure is really bad luck for any middle manager but some would say an avoidable situation if you competently lead your team. You may discover important reasons why this task has not been completed. Teacher stress, personal problems, disorganization or lack of commitment, all need your attention.

Nothing can be more morale building and heartening than receiving a letter from a parent congratulating you on the nature and ranges of homework your teachers have set. It does happen!

Strong leadership of curriculum areas creates a positive departmental ethos and one where staff feel supported and valued. It will bring about a committed workforce with sound professional relationships and reduce staff turnover. One rather frustrated and disillusioned Year 13 girl said of the Science Department:

> 'This is the fourth Physics teacher we've had since I started AS. The lack of continuity is, I feel, having a serious effect on my examination grades.'

A strong department is one where there are clear lines of communication, collaborative working practices and a collective desire to raise achievement by improving the quality of teaching and learning.

For many years there was a noticeable divide that separated the academic pillars of a school from its pastoral infrastructure. We then moved to a position where pastoral work was seen to underpin the work done in the curriculum areas. This slow but necessary evolution has now given rise to a system whereby pastoral work is no longer the sole responsibility of Year Managers and their tutor workforce but an obligation for all teachers to raise achievement and improve learning. Schools should now nurture an accepted partnership between these two aspects of school life.

Heads of Year are now referred to as Learning Managers or Directors of Learning and although the broad remit for pastoral care has become more of a collective responsibility, there are fundamental features of their job that directly influence the lives and personal happiness of pupils on a daily basis. One Year 8 succinctly reflected upon the work of his Year Head:

> 'Miss Clarke seems to know everything about us. She says she wants to get the best out of us. She's always around and takes an interest in everyone in the year and not just the ones who are naughty.'

The Head of Year should embody all that the school represents. Because comprehensive schools cater for large numbers of pupils there is a need to organize such populated establishments into manageable units. The Year or House System with their respective leaders is the way this is achieved. Year Leaders thus have a responsibility for the personal, social and academic development of the large group of pupils in their charge.

Year Leaders have a perceived status in the school – they have power and an ability to make things happen. This characteristic was alluded to by a rather lively Year 9 agent provocateur:

> 'I'd sooner be sent to the Head rather than Miss Mullvaney. He's soft. Just tell him what he wants to hear. Miss goes ballistic. You don't get on the wrong side of her.'

This quote would tend to give the uninitiated the impression that this school was regressing and that its Year Heads could all audition for the role of the PE teacher in the film *Kes*. However, comments from pupils in other schools about Year Managers were based upon similar feelings of loyalty and respect. Discipline is an acceptable code of behaviour and a framework in which certain attitudes are allowed to develop. The Head of Year does have a role in upholding acceptable behaviour just as much as other middle managers. It is, however, often the case that Year Heads are seen by pupils as wearing the routine disciplinary mantle. Some staff too, rather unwisely, judge the effectiveness of Year Heads by the standards of behaviour of their year group.

Year Heads do tend to filter serious breaches of discipline before handing the issue over to senior management. They do the groundwork and ensure that all the facts and paperwork are in place before either dealing with the situation themselves or referring to one of the leadership group.

> 'When I was beaten up by this Year 11 kid I was glad that Mr James, our Head of Year, dealt with it. He asked me lots

> of questions and seemed very concerned. He just took charge of everything and seemed to know exactly what to do.'

> 'I had a 20 pound note nicked from my coat in French. Our teacher sent for Mrs Bowden, our Head of Year. She got it back in about ten minutes. I overheard her telling him that he or the Head of Department should have sorted this out.'

Heads of Year should also be streetwise rather than connoisseurs of avenues and boulevards. Kids expect you to know what's going on outside the school gates as well as in the corridors and playgrounds. If you do not then they perceive this as a weakness. You need to be able to nip trouble in the bud before it starts or be able to tackle different situations in a confident and professional way. Your credibility in the year group suffers if you do not. A Year 10 with a penchant for skunk confided:

> 'My Head of Year don't know much. He found a shit pipe in my bag and he didn't have a clue. I fobbed him off, saying it was me little brother's that he used for blowing soap bubbles with.'

Pupils expect you to be confident and able to wear many hats. They feel you should be able to deal effectively with different tasks. You are someone who is seen to be approachable and does not flap. You will also be seen to work in partnership with your team of tutors and there is a close cooperation between you. Knowing the names of every person in your year group is also a prerequisite. After all, you expect them to know you and what you do. It does not look good when you walk into a tutor room and ask a pupil:

'Is Shiv Balasubramanian here this morning?'

The student replies with surprise:

'I'm Shiv, Sir.'

There will be occasions when your tutor will ask for help in dealing with a delicate or sensitive matter concerning one of your year. Such assistance is sought from you not just because of your status but also because of the professional and accomplished way you do your job. They recognize that you will know how to help. Heads of Year are frequently prime links in a chain of assistance for pupils and their families. Education Welfare, Social Services, Area Health Authority and specialist counselling services are all agencies with which you will be expected to liaise.

'Mrs Thomas [Head of Year] got my work permit sorted out for my evening job at the café by involving the man from Education Welfare. My Mum wasn't too sure about how many hours I could work and didn't want me overdoing it.'

'I got in trouble with the police and was charged with TDA [taking and driving away a motor vehicle]. I'd done this a few times. My Head of Year had to write a court report about how I was at school. Because he said I was making an effort with some of my lessons and that my attendance was OK the judge said he may give me a suspended sentence.'

In the majority of schools, persuading a PRU (Pupil Referral Unit) to take one of your pupils is similar to attempting to convince a vegan that rump steak is a root vegetable. After this pupil has set fire to the school, shot the Head teacher and systematically liberated all of the computers from the school's IT suite you may be in with a chance. It is vital that once the education programme and reintegration package have been identified, you do not abandon this student at the centre even though the rest of the staff consider them to be 'off-roll'. As you will be aware, they are certainly still on the school roll and remain the school's responsibility. The Head of Year is the key to avoiding such remarks as:

> 'Nobody from the school came to see me at the unit. I felt the school was glad to get rid of me and had dumped me here. They did not want me back.'

Year Managers play key roles in overseeing the academic progress of the pupils in their charge. They actively participate in target setting by liaising with the subject camps of the school and take significant responsibility for ensuring ARDs are purposeful and productive features on the school calendar. Your job, supported by your tutor team, is to act as achievement coordinator for the students in your year. Indeed, you are to recognize and reward all forms of achievement. This acknowledgement of success can take place in tutor time or during assembly. It is important to pupils.

> 'I really felt good about myself when Mrs Papadopoulos, our Head of Year, congratulated me on being selected to play in the county schools orchestra. She shook my hand on the school stage.'

> 'Some of our tutor group got mentioned in assembly for being the most improved over the term. I ain't never been mentioned in assembly before except in Year 8 when me and Delores had to stay behind for chewin'.'

Complementing your perceived status in the school, the Year Head should possess excellent communication skills. They are expected to be strong speakers whose assemblies are well presented and meaningful. Kids are quite disappointed if you are not talented on the oratory scene. Similarly, any newsletters or individual correspondence home should not be anaemic or of poor composition. One Year 7 parent told her son:

> 'I'd never met Mr Robbins but I spoke to him on the phone. It was a bit of a surprise, really. He seemed a bit quiet and ill at ease speaking to me. I suppose I expected someone more assertive and confident. But he was nice.'

In an effort to create an identity for your year, Year Managers should be perceived as energetic and motivational. The year activities you arrange and oversee will be as successful as an Ann Summers party without oestrogen if you appear lukewarm about the whole thing. As Tom Lehrer said about all things connected with teaching:

> 'Teaching is like a sewer. It's what you put into it that determines what comes out the other end.'

The quality of the middle management tier of any school provides the key to its success or failure. It is their enthusiastic participation and willingness to raise standards and achievement that reinforces the ethos and soul of the school. A measure of their success is how they are seen to lead a team of teachers to improve the quality of teaching and learning. How they interface with pupils along this journey is an integral part of this improvement and development process.

A summary of what the pupils say

1. We like to know who are the curriculum leaders in the school.
2. We'd like them to explain to us what they do.
3. We'd like to be able to see you directly if there is something bothering us and not always going through our tutors.
4. We'd like you to involve us in deciding what is a good lesson and how we best learn things.
5. Why not ask us some questions when you come in to observe our teacher? We can give you a good idea of what it's like in the lesson.
6. We prefer lessons when we can learn things and not when our teacher spends over half the time trying to control us. We'd like you to help them with their discipline problems.
7. Sometimes we get student teachers for a term and this is often unhelpful, particularly with exam classes.
8. We get bored if the work is too easy or there is not enough for us to do. It also does not help when the work set is too hard. We'd like work to be given us that is at our level but gives us some challenge.
9. We prefer to have a subject lesson in the same room rather than have to visit different ones.
10. We do like to see our work displayed in the classroom or around the school.
11. Many of us would like to join clubs or do extension work relating to your subject after school.
12. Can you explain to us about National Curriculum levels? Sometimes we don't think our teachers properly understand them.
13. Don't set us too many targets. We don't mind them but we get stressed too.

14 We do not like having too many teachers for a subject. You get used to one and then they leave.
15 We like it when Heads of Year give the year an identity as though we all belong.
16 We like healthy competition between groups and pupils.
17 We like Heads of Year to be seen as strong people but we also like them to be approachable if anyone needs help.
18 We like it when you recognize we have tried hard and achieved something.
19 We like to see you around the school at break times. It makes us feel safe.

6 Other personnel who impact on the pupil experience (1): The SENCO, PSHCE coordinator, careers coordinator

If I were ever asked the question 'Would you rather do ten rounds with Amir Khan or be appointed as a school Special Educational Needs Coordinator?' I feel my instant response would be to commit myself to the pugilistic alternative and await impending annihilation. My reluctance to take on the special educational needs (SEN) role is based upon the fact that I have always favoured a quick and agony free demise.

Because of the nature of the job, the school Special Educational Needs Coordinator (SENCO) will frequently feel bruised, harassed and battered by the people with whom they are expected to work in partnership. Head teachers will be sensitive to the position of their schools in league tables and also appear melancholic about budgets. The Local Education Authority, through the voices of its advisers and the Educational Psychologist (EP), will also bleat on about finite funding and resources. Indeed, these team-mates will on occasion disappoint you by making decisions that go against your wishes for a particular child. Engaging the help of learning and behaviour support teachers is like trying to recruit an endangered species.

You will be expected to liaise with other outside agencies such as occupational therapists, the child and adolescent mental health services, speech, language and the sensory support services as well as Connexions advisers. Your lot is not finished there. Frustrated by being required to cope with excessive bureaucracy, the SENCO will also work closely with Heads of Curriculum, Heads of Year, LSAs, parents and of course, if there's time, the pupils.

The quality and, indeed, quantity of SEN help for pupils is still, unfortunately, determined by where the pupil lives and the schools they attend. Statemented pupils will receive their Individual Education Programmes (IEPs) as a statutory right. However, despite the Code of Practice for SEN and the recommendations in the paper 'Every Child Matters', other children who are not in the statemented category, and who are deemed to have special needs, continue to be short-changed by the system. The SENCO and their band of LSAs will attempt to keep the show together. Their work will underpin the personalized learning programmes of those who have a greater degree of difficulty in learning than the majority of their age in mainstream education. Their clientele will also include the able, gifted and talented. There is a duty to meet their needs too by ensuring curriculum areas provide suitable extension and enrichment work.

The degree to which SEN pupils are allowed to participate in their educational provision is regarded by many as one of the most important factors in the success of any school SEN practice. There are, however, some students who may find such participation as being too onerous. They may have little self-insight and a lack of cognitive and communicative ability to discuss their perceived needs.

> 'I don't really understand what IEP business is all about. I know it's supposed to help me and all that. My Dad says what the school is doing is OK, so I suppose it must be good.'

Some SEN pupils are reluctant or unwilling to contribute to their learning programmes. One disaffected Year 10 pupil openly commented:

> 'Some lessons are boring and all this target setting non-sense means nothing at all. I can't wait to leave school.'

One key aspect for SEN pupils is their ability to build a trusting relationship with someone who is aware of their difficulties. In many cases this role is fulfilled by an LSA who has more daily contact with the student than any other adult in the school.

> 'I don't see Mrs Barnard [SENCO] much 'cos she's very busy. Miss Gupta [LSA] is good, though. She listens to me and we get on well. She lets me see the weekly report she does on me for Mrs Barnard. I trust her.'
>
> 'Mrs Ogunsalu [LSA] knows me best. I see her and she works with me most days. I can talk to her and she understands.'

Other relationships with LSAs may not be as productive:

> 'I thought I told Mrs Kennedy in confidence. At my annual review meeting [AR] all the people there started to ask me about it. I felt let down.'

SEN pupils are no different to their mainstream counterparts in that they too value teachers who are seen to be approachable and take a broader interest in their lives. Teachers and support staff who forge honest and positive relationships with pupils will receive back from them reliable and truly representative information.

It is also no surprise how philosophical some students can be about the whole process of consultation. A classic example was given by a Year 9 pupil on the subject of target setting:

> 'I felt there was really no point in me being at the meeting with Mr Sood [SENCO], Miss Boyle [LSA] and my parents. The teachers had already set me my targets and they were just read out to me. My Mum said the purpose of the meeting was for discussing my progress and for us all to plan the next term.'

Similarly, ARs can be seen as just tokenism and which give little opportunity for negotiation to take place. Some pupils have concerns about not being in control regarding what is written about their reviews. One student felt his views had been misinterpreted by the SENCO. This experience was counterbalanced by two pupils who, quite independent of each other, put the success of their ARs and progress meetings down to shared and negotiated decision making. The necessary gauging of their views took place prior to the meeting and had been accurately recorded by the children's LSAs.

One student commented that his formal review meeting was a rather depressing experience:

> 'I felt it did nothing for my self-confidence. I felt it just went on about my weaknesses and drew attention to them.'

Another pupil claimed a more positive experience. Her comments related to her IEP:

> 'My teacher [SENCO] explained things in words easy for me to understand. She said it in what my Mum called "child speak". My Mum and I were both happy because the way ahead for me would be broken down into chunks that I would be able to manage.'

SENCOs work in both a supportive and an advisory capacity on curriculum areas. They help develop areas of the curriculum and schemes of work to become more consumer friendly for SEN pupils. Most departments have an SEN link teacher whose role is to tap expertise. Statemented pupils receive priority and do well from this liaison. The non-statemented student who has SEN frequently does not fare so well. This is not a deliberate act but just that there is insufficient time and limited resources to fulfil everyone's individual needs.

SENCOs not only cope with being pulled in all directions by school staff, the LEA and specialist support teams but also face considerable parental microscopy. Pushy parents, obsessive parents, irrational and unreasonable parents all contribute to the daily hypertension of the SENCO. They often find themselves in the middle of grievances or asked to mediate and find acceptable and practical solutions. In short, the Parents' Charter with its well-intentioned philosophy frequently asks SENCOs to achieve the impossible. A rather arrogant Year 10 girl, whose manner suggested she was a parental clone, made the point:

> 'My parents say I have dyslexia and that the school has done very little to help me. They demanded a consultation with the Educational Psychologist and Mr Antonides [SENCO] has refused to get me a meeting. They have no confidence in this man or the school and are now going to get me a private assessment.'

My heartfelt sympathies go out to Mr Antonides and other SENCOs.

*

Personal, Social, Health and Citizenship Education (PSHCE) programmes in schools are rather like bidets.

Everyone feels they are worth having but nobody quite knows how best to use them. Indeed, the success of PSHCE is governed by the willingness of schools to place emphasis on this programme package and to justify its standing alongside the formal curriculum.

For years schools have tinkered with PSHCE courses. Some were initially delivered as a ragbag of curricular loose ends by tutors who frequently felt out of their comfort zones. Much welcome progress has been made over the years concerning content and development of PSHCE. Many schools now boast programmes of study implemented by specialist teams of committed staff. Their common aim is for the young people in their charge to develop into healthy, informed and responsible adults. Many establishments have introduced the use of highly effective focus days with relevant material presented by professionals who have in-depth knowledge of the subject matter.

The credibility of PSHCE with the Year 7 to Year 13 proletariat will be geared by a number of factors. The school has overall control over these criteria. Schools who deliver PSHCE through the tutor period programme frequently run into problems. Tutors complain about their lack of suitability to teach the course components. Kids pick up on this fragility and make comments:

> 'Miss appeared a bit uncomfortable talking about alcohol and she couldn't answer all of our questions.'
>
> 'My teacher seemed out of her depth with this topic.'

They also spot teachers who attempt to blag their way through a lesson and ramble on about a topic about which they have a sketchy appreciation:

> 'Sir is a young French teacher. What does he know about teaching *Crime and Punishment*?'

> 'I object to being told things about drugs by someone who clearly knows little about the subject.'

A sharp and rather disillusioned Year 11 boy reflected on his tutor's rather uninspiring and colourless lesson:

> 'You could tell he hadn't prepared the lesson. He carped on for a while and then gave us a worksheet, which we couldn't do because he'd forgotten the accompanying video.'

We infer from the above responses that if PSHCE is given a low priority by staff then the pupils will give it similar treatment.

> 'Our tutor periods swing between doing absolutely nothing at all and then one day he will suddenly talk to us about study skills.'

> 'Sometimes I'm sure she is thinking "What's the point of all this?" Someone should tell her that with her attitude, we think that too.'

One final quote from a Year 11 student, destined to be a Queen's Counsel, unimpressed by five years of rather lukewarm PSHCE lessons:

> 'I trust the Maths teacher who teaches me Maths but I do not share the same confidence in the Maths teacher who teaches me PSHCE.'

Students do want PSHCE lessons to work. They do want to talk about issues relevant to them. They do welcome opportunities for debate. They do want to learn about the society in which they live.

> 'It was a great session. The outside speaker kept us all busy and we felt he was really interested in us because he gave us time to chat about our ideas and opinions.'
>
> 'It was useful listening to someone who has a real knowledge of the subject. The leaflets they gave us backed up what they had spoken about and we placed them in our PSHCE folders.'

Even if schools stay away from the use of outside speakers, the pupils find it helpful when someone other than their tutor delivers the topic:

> 'It's good not having the same teacher like our tutor for PSHCE lessons. You can't expect them to be able to talk about some of the things we need to know. Having someone else who seems to be confident in what they're teaching gives a fresh approach to the subject.'

Comments similar to these would seem to vindicate the use of specialist teams to teach certain topics. I happened to hear snapshots of tutor PSHCE lessons also supporting this concept and practice.

One quite enthusiastic tutor who was talking to his Year 12 tutor group about poverty and deprivation apparently made the classic faux pas:

> 'Look guys, homelessness is homelessness. I don't care where you live.'

We are all guilty of similar dumb statements in the course of our teaching career. To give another example, I was observing a PSHCE parenting lesson with Year 11. The teacher, whose communicative skills had never been in question before, suddenly came out with a classic that could easily have been attributed to Homer Simpson:

'And don't forget, lads. Having a baby is the most strenuous thing known to man.'

A PSHCE programme needs good marketing to staff and the pupils. Sufficient training of staff and a generous allocation of relevant resources should naturally follow when a school gives PSHCE a senior position on the timetable. Its transfer to the children should be by enthusiastic and informed teaching.

The management and development of such subject material should fall into the lap of the PSHCE coordinator. This vacancy is, hopefully, filled by someone who believes in PSHCE, and subsequently leads the school into delivering a resolute and effective programme. It is often the case, however, that the position of responsibility is filled by someone who has it thrust upon them. It's a post that is frequently viewed as playing pass the parcel with Semtex. Very few people are willing to peel away the final wrapping and find they are now custodians of this potentially troublesome prize.

In an attempt to give this PSHCE curriculum greater kudos and credibility the majority of schools issue students with portfolios for them to assemble and catalogue the work they undertake in this subject. Some schools assess the efficacy of the course by tests and examinations. Teachers may have different feelings and opinions about PSHCE. In the current teaching climate there is a common view that we are being asked to shoulder more and more. New initiatives seem to appear with alarming regularity each month. Many of us just want to be left alone to get on with our classroom teaching. Nevertheless, the majority of us entered the profession because somewhere in our nervous system there was a centre which cares about kids and the way we can contribute to making their experience of school more relevant and meaningful. At the risk of sounding too cheesy and over-mozzarellaring the pizza, if we don't make an effort to help them leave school as informed and responsible citizens then who will?

One grateful Year 11 student concluded his personal statement for his record of achievement portfolio with the following words:

> 'I have enjoyed my life at secondary school. It has given me confidence, knowledge and a sense of responsibility. I now leave my childhood years behind and look forward to a life of adultery.'

*

Running as part of any PSHCE schedule will be a careers education and guidance programme. The reference manual for this essential provision is the 'National Framework for Careers Education and Guidance'. This document sets out the learning outcomes for 11 to 19 year olds as they journey through the National Curriculum key stages. Its intention is to provide young people with enough career management skills so they are prepared for the decision making and challenges at the end of Years 9, 11 and 13. Complementing and running parallel with such a programme is the Connexions service. It offers students the opportunity to access personal advisers who help steer young people through the minefields of their teenage years. They are able to offer young people wide-ranging advice from housing to training routes and courses.

Careers guidance in schools is the responsibility of the student services teacher. They help prepare and coordinate programmes of study that address the identified needs of pupils at the three key stages. It is important that such material is not seen as a bolt-on activity and uses materials that are developmentally appropriate.

The activities and learning outcomes must be monitored and evaluated to ensure the mechanism is meeting the needs of both students and other stakeholders. Pupils value a well-resourced careers reference room. Some schools designate part of their library facilities to careers education. The ability to access the 'careers teacher' was regarded by pupils as important. One Year 9 girl claimed the careers suite in the school was:

> 'An intimidating place to be. Filled with Year 13 pupils. I'm too scared to go in there.'

Another Key Stage 3 pupil remarked:

> 'It's full of university stuff. I want to be an electrician.'

Students did applaud the increase in the number of information access points. Computer, internet facilities and school email networks made information access and retrieval easier for students. One enterprising Year 11 pupil who appeared only too ready to leave in the summer commented:

> 'I got all the information I needed about day release from doing a Google.'

Students also valued the use of guest speakers, careers markets and expos.

At Key Stage 4, work experience takes place much to the annoyance of subject teachers, who are attempting to cover GCSE syllabus material in a limited time period. The majority of students with whom I have discussed this adventure see it as enjoyable and worthwhile. It did help them gain insight into both the glamorous and the unexciting aspects of the world of work. Many wanted as much emphasis placed upon preparing them for this encounter as there was for evaluating the experience.

> 'I thought my Aunty Leah was a stroppy person but you don't half meet some worse than her when you're serving in a shoe shop on a Saturday!'

At one work experience debriefing session, a Year 11 young man with the reasoning powers of Descartes reflected on his two weeks at a large retail company:

> 'If you studied promotion there, all of the senior positions were occupied by men. An absolutely deplorable state of affairs and an unequivocal insult to the female gender, don't you think, Sir?'

A summary of what the pupils say

1. Us SEN pupils who have not been statemented still need to be given time and attention. Sometimes we feel a bit left out.
2. IEPs should be given to us in child friendly language and also in manageable chunks so that it doesn't appear too much for us.
3. We like to be given a say in compiling our IEP.
4. We would like to be able to build a trusting relationship with an adult who can truly represent our feelings at ARs or progress meetings.
5. We would like to feel that if we tell something in confidence (child protection things excluded) that we could trust that person not to let everyone know.
6. Can our teachers consult with us before they set our targets?
7. Don't forget us students who are called the able,

gifted and talented. Sometimes the enrichment and extension work is inappropriate.

8 Can our teachers be given help in setting suitable work for SEN pupils?
9 If we are to study PSHCE can we be consulted about how the programme will be delivered?
10 Can we be consulted about the contents and relevance of parts of the course?
11 If teachers are seen to be apathetic about PSHCE and give it a low priority then so will we.
12 Can you make sure that teachers know what they are talking about in PSHCE? We sometimes feel they flounder with certain topics.
13 Can you check the quality of outside speakers before you let them loose on us? Some are extremely boring and don't know how to pitch to young people.
14 Some of us feel that we need more information and guidance from the Connexions service about what jobs and courses are available for us when we leave school.
15 We enjoy work experience but would like just as much time in preparing us for it as is spent in reviewing how it went.

7 Other personnel who impact on the pupil experience (2): the Head teacher, cover teachers, caretaker, groundsperson

> 'I never see him.'

This most common reply from pupils applies to the Head teacher.

> 'Well, he does the odd assembly and speaks at parents' meetings, I suppose, but you don't see him other than that,' added a member of Year 10.

People become Head teachers because they are passionate about making a difference to the lives of young people. They want the pupils in their schools to receive a high standard of education and for them to be successful learners. Their students are to become confident individuals, responsible citizens and effective contributors to society. Tell that to any 13 year old or interview panel and they would be impressed. However, you would receive the reply from the teenager:

> 'Mmm. But I never see him.'

Head teachers are judged by performance criteria. These national benchmarks have been developed by leadership organizations to give clear guidance to Head teachers and prospective school principals about what is expected from them in the job. These measurable criteria would include their showing clear vision and principles, an ability to demonstrate strategic planning and having the capacity to influence others. They should also be seen as effective communicators and competent individuals who are able to manage change. Within this leadership and management dimension they are to be both trustworthy and credible figures.

To pupils, Head teachers are people who are in charge of the school and are the bosses of the teachers in that learning environment. They view them as figures of authority, the top disciplinarians and the ones who deal with the media. They are also seen as busy people and often not in school. They are the staff who set the standards of teaching, uniform and behaviour. They write letters home to parents about concerts, important dates, new school building projects, cuts in school buses and changes to school dinner arrangements. Head teachers, in students' eyes, are people who can hire and fire teachers, bleat on for hours in assembly and prize days about examination passes and seem neurotic about budgets.

A rather disaffected Year 11 girl disclosed this sentence between puffs of a cigarette:

> 'She always is having her photograph taken with some nob from the Council or local papers.'

To supplement her particular take on the Head teacher's meetings with the press or dignitaries, she also mentioned that the school received a facelift on these occasions together with naughty students being removed from corridors and lessons.

Another recalcitrant from the same year added:

> 'I've only met Mrs Lewis once and that's when she excluded me for swearing at a teacher.' (The Head teacher's surname was, in fact, Lewin.)

A fellow Year 11 girl with a more utilitarian take on this demanding role said in defence of her Head teacher:

> 'It must be a big responsibility making sure that all teachers are doing what they are supposed to be doing. They've also got to spend lots of money wisely otherwise we don't get any textbooks or supply teachers.'

A Year 7 complete with new blazer and optimism was full of praise and admiration for his new Head teacher's work:

> 'Mrs Rashid is a very important person and she has a very busy job. She's paid thousands of pounds as well.'

The Head teacher is, to many pupils, the ultimate disciplinary force. Indeed, I worked with one Head who ran the school like a Roman general. Few pupils crossed him. I was in his office one lunchtime and partway through a conversation he suddenly leapt up from his chair and opened the glass door that led onto the main road.

> 'Just a second,' he said. 'I've just seen this lad with no tie on, his shirt hanging out and wearing trainers!'

He then proceeded to stop the young man and give him an almighty verbal salvo about standards of dress and setting a poor example to the local community. At the height of the Head's rubicund and frenzied vocal assault, the young man retaliated by shouting:

> 'Look, bugger off, mate. I'm 17 and I don't even go to your flamin' school!'

For serious breaches of school discipline Head teachers decide the magnitude of the punishment. It can, therefore, come as a shock when the kids feel the punishment does not fit the crime:

> 'Angelo Pettifer is always in trouble. He gets away with loads of things. The Head should have kicked him out long ago.'

Some troublesome pupils indicate they have been warned about their behaviour and the possible involvement of the Head teacher. Their poor conduct continued only to find that when they eventually reached the Head teacher's office, there was anticlimax: an admonishment or a reprimand, yet nothing to give them cause for concern. A Year 10, whose school career was peppered with felonies, spoke in a derisory way about his Head teacher:

> 'I've seen her more times than I can remember. I ain't scared of her. I get a bollockin' and maybe a three-day exclusion. Big thrills!'

A boy in the same year seemed quite horrified at this pupil's punishment:

> 'I don't know what you have to do in this school to be permanently excluded. He should have gone, back in Year 9. It's almost as though the Head is scared of him.'

Pupils say they expect to be punished for wrongdoings. If ever insubordination reaches the attention of the Head teacher they are quite prepared for the Full

Monty. If it does not happen then they perceive this as a weakness. They sensibly view the involvement of the Head teacher as the last link in the disciplinary chain. On occasions, the reality for them is that the chain seems to have recurrent final links.

I spoke at length with a school council who were all in agreement that they would like their Head teacher to have a higher profile around the school. Their cogent argument contained statements such as:

> 'It would be good for pupil morale.'
> 'It would be good for teachers' morale.'
> 'The Head would really know what is going on in his/her school.'
> 'It would be good for school discipline.'
> 'They would experience good and bad lessons.'

A member of Year 13 claimed her misanthropic perspective of her school was fuelled by the Head teacher:

> 'In assembly he crowed on about my charity efforts bringing praise from the local community. Trouble was, he mentioned me by name twice and both times he got it wrong. What do you expect? He's a "virtual head". He's never spoken to me in six years.'

Pupils appreciate that the Head teacher has many hats to wear. They fully understand their huge financial responsibilities and realize the job is split between business and educational roles. They also endorse the recommendation that the appointment of a business manager would go a long way in giving a Head more time to influence teaching and learning. Some students go as far as saying that the Deputy Head teachers seem to keep the school running on a daily basis.

Appointing a business manager who would manage

the school budget, deal with bureaucracy, take responsibility for maintaining school premises and manage long-term development projects would probably cut down Head teachers' workload by over one-third. This would go some way to allowing them the daily contact with students that both parties see as an essential requirement.

The principle that learning should be at the heart of strategic planning and resource management features in the catechism of most Head teachers. Trying to secure funding for new school buildings is a time consuming and skilful process. Pupils are usually unaware of such efforts and difficulties and continue to complain of their dilapidated Technology block. On a winter's day they all moan about the Spartan conditions and they're all feeling a cold wind blowing from the Urals (though probably it was the urinals in one school where I worked). It must be of little consolation and comfort to any Head when, after years of chasing grants, fund raising, letters to the DCSF (Department for Children, Schools and Families) and hours of meetings and negotiations, they manage to secure the green light for the new block, only to hear some Year 9 analyst say:

> 'About time an' all!'

No wonder there is a shortage of Head teachers.

Heads seek continual improvement for their schools. One Head teacher arranged a residential weekend away for school middle leaders. During one session on development and planning he actively encouraged some 'blue skies' thinking. It was rather ironic that one Monday morning some two weeks later, the Head of Art reported to the Head teacher a newfound opportunity for blue skies thinking in his department. Thieves had stripped the copper roof from the two Art buildings. Blue skies, and in the middle of February!

Some Heads possess better powers of verbal communication than others. Pupils expect the Head teacher to be confident orators and to speak with clarity and strength. Any soul who does not produce the goods while speaking in public is viewed as anaemic, not fully in control and someone who cannot cut the mustard. A rather voluble member of a sixth form compared two Head teachers she had witnessed perform in public during her school years:

> 'The first one we had always gave tremulous talks in assemblies and public meetings. He just did not give the impression of being comfortable and confident with speaking to large numbers of people. He would pause between sentences almost as though he couldn't think of what words to use next. We would describe him as experiencing "call waiting mode". The head we have now is the complete opposite. When he speaks, everyone listens and is impressed by his fluency and gravitas.'

Many pupils are also concerned about poor teaching and a Head teacher's apparent reluctance to do anything about the situation. Pupils feel that if enough concern is shown about instances of protracted poor teaching then there should be a fairly rapid remedy. Often any improvement can take some time, with middle managers given the responsibility for investigating and monitoring the situation. Students are unaware of the necessary protocol and procedure and they may sometimes lose faith in a Head teacher if they appear not to have personally taken control.

> 'He can act quick when he wants'

was the vehement observation of a Year 11 pupil about the powers of his school's Head teacher. He then continued:

> 'When that teacher touched up that Year 7 kid, he soon disappeared from the school. Our class has been complaining about Mr Jellicoe's English lessons for ages but nothing's been done.'

Another similar and quite justified concern was made about Head teachers and lesson observations:

> 'If she came in to our lessons more she could really understand how bad Mr Fenner's lessons are. He seems to clean up his act when he's being observed but then things go back to normal next lesson.'

A pessimistic view concerning the dearth of Chemistry teachers was expressed by a senior pupil:

> 'I know there's a shortage of Chemistry teachers but I really feel the Head panicked when he took on Mr Abbas. He doesn't know any Chemistry.'

Pupils have noted the increase in the number of lesson observations as schools have journeyed further along the road of self-evaluation. As one classroom-wise pupil reminded me:

> 'It was only in Year 7 when we thought that teachers were coming in to our lessons to look at us. We all know now that they're looking at the teacher. At the end of the lesson with Mr Logan, Evita Littlewood called out, "How many marks did he give you for that lesson, Sir? We all reckon seven out of ten!"'

Fewer people in teaching these days are happy to take on the demanding role of Headship. We may be moving towards models never before countenanced such as shared Headships, distributed leadership or federations. Whatever the remedy, pupil opinion will continue to play an important touchstone in measuring the job success of school leaders.

*

The use of cover supervisors (CSs) in lessons has helped reduce the burden on teaching staff for covering the lessons of their absent colleagues. Cover supervisors are required to undertake such cover for short-term absences. The pupils seem to notice they are used far too often in some schools.

> 'Our Head of Year takes us for History and his lessons are always being taken by a cover teacher when he's called away to deal with something.'

A common problem, once more highlighted by the kids, is that cover teachers often arrive at lessons without any work set by the absent teacher. Pupils say that they are often set 'noddy' work to do that does not tie into or match the topic they are currently studying.

> 'I felt sorry for the geezer. He come into the classroom expecting to find the work on the desk. He then started to ask us what we'd been doing and set us some work from the textbook. We then pointed out that Sir had our books. It was a waste of a lesson, really.'

The degree of effectiveness of a lesson covered by a CS lies in their ability to maintain control of the class and also the suitability of the work set by the teacher. Many pupils say that some CSs struggle to manage behaviour and that little work is achieved. Cover teachers are supposed to receive at least three days' training on all aspects of their supervisory role including how to deal with classroom disruption. One Year 9 girl spoke of her frustration:

> 'We did need a bit of help with the work but Miss couldn't really help because she was too busy controlling some naughty boys in our group.'

Pupils say that some cover staff are helpful and seem to know enough about the work to be able to assist the students and answer their questions. A conscientious member of Year 8 had the same CS twice in one day:

> 'She was great in our Geography lesson and she helped us with our map work. In the afternoon we had her for Maths. She'd never heard of tessellations and she tried to turn up the volume on the video with my calculator. She thought it was the remote control.'

As their title suggests, cover supervisors are to supervise the lesson and to issue and collect work that has been set by the absent teacher. It must be extremely frustrating for them not to be able to deal with the children's questions. It can also be quite humiliating and degrading for them when some insensitive staff make disparaging remarks about them to the children:

> 'Mr Parker made a snide remark about the man who took us for his lesson. He said he wasn't a proper English teacher anyway.'

Cover teachers often have to oversee practical subjects. There is an obvious drawback here because they are not qualified to allow the students to participate in such 'hands-on' activities. The air of creativity is sadly lost from the lesson. Theory work or watching a video is the substitute exercise. However, in some PE lessons, both supervision and teaching were witnessed and amusingly reported:

> 'Sir [the CS] told me to come off my line when Shola crossed the ball. I knew I hadn't a hope of catching it. It went right over the top of me head and Sanjay nodded it in. I felt a right idiot. Great advice, Sir!'

A worrying use of LSAs or teaching assistants as CSs will give rise to palpable problems. One SEN pupil in Year 8 complained:

> 'Mrs Hussain spent most of the time trying to get some of the girls in the group to do some work. I only saw her for a few minutes.'

Cover supervisors have their own concerns and these are not far removed from the issues underlined by the pupils. Constant poor behaviour, a lack of work or inappropriate work set are their principal worries. They are also anxious not to be seen as treading on the toes of LSAs in their efforts to assist those pupils who need help. Sometimes, however, CSs feel they are forced to teach and not just supervise because of the inadequacy and nature of the work that has been left. Negative comments from teachers about their status and efforts have unmistakable effects on their morale and confidence.

*

An exercise asking pupils to describe the characteristics of the school caretaker seemed to elicit a host of similar adjectives. Common descriptors were sulky, bad tempered, grumpy, miserable and child hating. The curmudgeon stereotype was reinforced by numerous anecdotes all illustrating an individual who may have a picture of King Herod or The Pied Piper of Hamlin on their office wall.

> 'He's not very friendly.'
>
> 'All he does is lock the toilets.'
>
> 'She's got a huge bunch of keys and all she does is watch the CCTV screen.'

The caretaker's lot does seem to engender rather biased and unfair criticism from the pupils. Caretakers are on the receiving end of poor pupil behaviour in a school. Towel dispensers set alight, graffiti on walls, chewing gum on floors, litter, broken windows and furniture repairs are just a few of their weekly chores. Their work often picks up the pieces of the seedy side of secondary school life. Some staff too give them a hard time. Cleaning staff can be furious about the way classrooms are left and furniture is treated.

One pleasant and rational young lady in Year 10 spoke about the toilet situation:

> 'Locking the toilets in lesson times is inhuman. I know we have got some irresponsible people in the school whose behaviour spoils it for others. What about our basic human rights? My friend nearly poohed herself last week. She had to go to find a member of staff to unlock the loos for her. It was degrading.'
>
> 'There's never any soap and toilet paper.'

In reply to the toilets dilemma, a frustrated and angry concierge felt exhausted about soap issues. His relentless feelings of exasperation in dealing with the constant problem, together with a lack of support from senior staff, was probably responsible for this curious linguistic statement:

> 'I'm fed up with this stealing of soap business. It's like déjà vu all over again.'

An example of a caretaker in bellicose mood, and deeply paranoid about certain pupils with a reputation for disorderly conduct, happened in a school in North London. The caretaker was passing a classroom and saw a Year 11 pupil playing with the classroom blinds. The school keeper's immediate verbal command was:

> 'Get orf them blinds, Mancini! Leave 'em alone!'

The young sociopath's reply was:

> 'You can't tell me off, Garner. I've got a disability.'

Mr Garner's scepticism and enquiring mind forced him to question the young man:

> 'Oh, yer. And what disability have you got, then?'
>
> 'I've got Tourette's . . . So f**k off!'

exclaimed the petulant Mancini.

One school welcomed its school keeper to one of its assemblies. He spoke about the nature of his job and included some of the unpleasant things his team have to do because of the thoughtless behaviour of some youngsters in the school. It was well received by the pupils, many saying they never really knew what were the caretaker's duties. The talk helped him feel more accepted and less of a grumpy alien. School and year councils are currently promoting similar bridge building exercises.

*

Students rarely meet up with personnel who tend football and hockey pitches. Cricket squares are neatly manicured and athletics tracks appear with meticulous regularity after the Easter break. There has been only one occasion when I have known pupils to actively seek the company of a groundsperson and that was to pour scorn on his handiwork. The gentleman in question had white-lined the athletics track and during sports day that year, each participant of the 100 metres race from Year 7 to Year 11 broke the existing school record. The Head teacher praised the new Head of PE for her tremendous efforts with a previously moribund group of competitors. A suspicious track official from the Chemistry Department dampened the hysteria and adulation when he paced the distance as 93 metres. It transpired that the groundsperson's parsimony with his chalk mixture was due to a sudden downpour of rain and also a sudden telephone call from his wife demanding she should be taken to ASDA.

A summary of what the pupils say

1. We'd like Head teachers to have more of a visible presence around the school.
2. We feel an increased presence of the Head would contribute to maintaining the school ethos.
3. We'd like our Head teacher to be more approachable and accessible.

4 We expect our Head teacher to know our names when you have to speak with us.
5 We'd like you to employ a business manager to help you run the non-educational side of your job so that you have more time for knowing what really goes on in your school.
6 We don't feel that discipline is a dirty word. We would like you to deal more effectively with pupils who are constantly disruptive.
7 We don't want you to break your promises and if you say you are going to do something then we expect you to do it.
8 We expect you to be a good communicator. If you are not it affects your credibility with us.
9 We'd like you to visit our lessons more often so that you can sample the quality of teaching and how much we learn.
10 We'd like you to act on poor teaching as quickly as possible.
11 We'd like you to consult us on issues that directly affect us to seek our ideas and views on best practices. This consultation should not be just confined to the school council.
12 We want you to lead by example.
13 We don't want you to be always obsessed with examination results and league tables. We like to be valued as people as well as examination statistics.
14 We'd like you to continue to improve the home/school partnership so that our parents understand more about our learning.
15 Can cover supervisors be given more training in behaviour management?
16 Can teachers who are absent from school set us work that is both relevant and appropriate? Sometimes we

have to ask the cover teachers lots of questions and they don't always know the answers.

17 Some of our classes have more than their fair share of cover teachers. Are all of these cover lessons really necessary?

18 We'd like to work in partnership with the caretaker so that we can both discuss common issues. We want to make the school a better place too.

19 We'd like the school keeper and their team to know that we are not all vandals and troublemakers.

8 The curriculum

> 'Now I don't want you to worry, class. These tests will have no effect on your grades. They merely determine your future social status and financial success. If any.'
>
> Bart Simpson's teacher.
> Jon Vitti, *The Simpsons*, Fox TV, 1990

It would seem that our cartoon friend is also a victim of a dubious testing system that is not fit for purpose.

Both pupils and their parents cite the unremitting demands of national tests as the most common cause of pupil stress. A group of Year 10 students spoke of Year 8 as being the perfect year because of the absence of national testing. However, some teachers may point to the noticeable dip in Year 8 pupil performance in this 'limbo year' being caused by there being no focus and an absence of such tests.

Children undertake national tests from Key Stage 1 through to Key Stage 5. They are even assessed at the Foundation Stage, formerly Key Stage 0. Politicians seem obsessed with testing and I can foresee gene technology being used to test at the foetal stage and these results being used in hospital league tables.

Many students feel that testing is something that has to be done. Indeed, they have grown up with it and know little else. One Year 9 pupil reflected quite openly about his schooling:

> 'I suppose you've got to have these tests to see how well you are doing but it all gets a bit much sometimes. Before

> the tests there's warm-up or practice tests and some of our teachers get quite on edge about them. Some of my mates do too.'

Another student in Year 7 felt some injustice about the testing process:

> 'My primary school was a great place. I really enjoyed it there and the teachers were good. Our SATs [Standard Attainment Tests] results apparently put us nowhere near the top in the league tables. I don't know whether that means we were crap or our teachers. My Dad said it meant the school.'

A Year 7 from the same stable indicated that many of her friends felt under enormous pressure at Key Stage 2 tests:

> 'We all thought that these tests we were doing would affect our chances of going to the secondary school we wanted. Our teachers said they wouldn't but my Mum said they would.'

A judicious Year 11 girl pondered over the purpose behind the Key Stage 3 English tests:

> 'Some of my friends were not entered for the Shakespeare paper. I mean, what are these tests for, assessing the school or its students?'

Key Stage 3 testing was also interpreted by some as having a relevance to option choices and core subject setting in Year 10. Equally many pupils find them an unnecessary inconvenience and completely irrelevant to their Key Stage 4 opportunities.

> 'I hate these test things,'

quoted one Year 10 boy, who had the vocabulary repertoire of Long John Silver's parrot. 'I hate writing and I hate giving long answers.' Surprisingly, the words 'pieces of eight!' did not feature in his pessimistic riposte.

On the other end of the agreeability spectrum, a fellow Year 10 girl stressed that she found the tests they took in Year 9 to be clearly presented, quite straightforward and consumer friendly:

> 'I know I was very nervous about doing these SATs. We all were. They weren't too bad, really, because the questions were clear and not out to trick you.'

One thing about most kids is that they are competitive and if they have been tested on something they will be anxious to know how they have fared. Results given in National Curriculum levels are wonderful if you have to complete your school PANDA (Performance and Assessment Data) but to Astrid in Year 9, discovering she is attainment level 6 in English and a level 5 in Science is of little value. Knowing she may be average for the group is some consolation. Talking to your bottom band Year 9s, however, about attainment levels within attainment targets is also as inane as telling them a joke in Latvian.

The whole issue of testing needs a radical overhaul if we are to improve teaching and learning. We owe this to our pupils. We owe this to our teachers. Written external tests dominate the curriculum. They are tests that cannot embody and reflect some of the important aims of education. Genuine learning is not always truly reflected by the testing of pupils particularly when they are focused solely on getting grades or levels. Learning to learn is in danger of becoming less important than doing well in tests.

A low ability Year 10 pupil who had already shouldered a wealth of testing from primary school to Key Stage 3 in secondary told me of his loss of motivation:

> 'I know I'm not very good. Trouble is, I keep finding this out. It don't do nothing for my confidence.'

Putting national testing to one side, there is clearly room for a partnership between formative and summative assessment that will give the most effective feedback to students about their current performance and potential. Pupils really seem to value one-to-one sessions with teachers and also constructive written comments in their reports. A Year 11 girl endorsed this opinion:

> 'It's good for me, and I suppose good for my parents too, to be able to talk with my subject teachers about how I'm doing. It's more personal and meaningful than just a grade on a piece of paper.'

The introduction of a National Curriculum in the late 1980s insisted on a common curriculum for schools that covered nine areas of learning and experience. For those new to teaching, still in embryo at that time, these areas included the aesthetic and creative, human and social, linguistic and literary, mathematical, moral, physical, spiritual, scientific and technological. Within these areas four elements of learning were to be cultivated. These were knowledge, concepts, skills and attitudes. Within the framework of this curriculum there were to be four key characteristics. Again, for those of us with amnesia or who have just had the most unpleasant teaching day possible, they were breadth, balance, relevance and differentiation.

If you ask pupils today about their curricular diet, well over three-quarters of them will say that they want their lessons to be more interesting and fun. This does nothing more than re-emphasize the criticism that the narrow focus of tests creates a limited curriculum. Pupils see a blinkered view of the relevance of the curriculum. This is a direct assault on one of the key characteristics of the National Curriculum proposals. Both the academically successful and the disaffected students say they are not enjoying their lessons as much as they should.

> 'I can't see the point of a lot of the stuff we are taught,' said a Year 10 boy. 'I don't think I'll ever use a lot of the facts that are thrown at me. I mean, who wants to know that caesium is an alkali metal? Like I'll need that in thirty years' time? Not!'

Pupils seem to want more visible messages about the relevance of the curriculum to their daily and future lives. They want real life connections with vocational and practical applications. One example of a Year 11 Geography lesson that seemed to go down well with the troops was given by a girl who displayed an initial lukewarm commitment to the subject:

> 'I only took Geography because there was nothing else really that appealed to me in that option column. We had a great lesson when Miss invited a surveyor in to speak with us. He really tied together lots of the things we'd learned in Geography, Science and Maths. He also told us that he has to write lots of reports and that he'd found the English at school a help.'

It is this awareness of connections across the curriculum, recognizing continuity and progression, that adds to the relevance of the curriculum for the pupils.

Enjoyment of the curriculum does seem to wane as we journey through the key stages. By the end of Year 9 youngsters experience a real low point and this may well be compounded by an absence of subject choice. There seems to be a lift in their spirits and motivation in Year 10 when they feel they are given some degree of liberty and autonomy in choosing subjects.

> 'I was glad to drop History. It didn't do much for me. Doing Business Studies and GCSE PE in Year 10 made me feel more positive about school.'

Some critics argue that the National Curriculum, and all the tinkering and refinement that have been associated with it over the years, remains outdated and is focused on knowledge transmission rather than knowledge transformation. Its confined and repetitive curriculum implies we are producing individuals who may be good at passing tests but are less competent at applying their knowledge and skills to other situations. Our teachers help their pupils to secure champagne performances from a lemonade curriculum.

Increasing the breadth and range of course choice would promote a degree of personalized learning and would be welcomed by students from Key Stage 4 onwards. It is anticipated that the introduction of work related diplomas would help in this dimension, providing there is the expertise to successfully deliver these courses.

In terms of breadth and balance of the curriculum pupils notice the bias towards English, Maths and Science but the majority regard it as relevant and appropriate. Even the most recalcitrant of pupils in Year 9 made the following remark:

> 'My Dad says if I'm to help him with his landscaping business he wants me to do more than push a 'barrow. He's not too good at doing written estimates, invoices and all that reading lark. He wants me to do it.'

The Modern Foreign Languages teacher who asked a Year 9 pupil for the meaning of the expression 'J'ai grand faim' and received the reply 'I've got a big wife' must feel comfortable with the decision that languages are no longer compulsory at Key Stage 4. On the other hand, the Key Stage 2 teacher must be yelling 'curriculum overload!' with the decision to include languages in primary schools. Less able students are dropping languages which they clearly perceive as too hard. A pragmatic Year 9 pupil who hailed from Canning Town in London's East End told me:

> 'If I walked down the East India Dock Road I'd hear Bengali. I don't think I've ever seen a French bloke. Why am I learning French?'

Similarly, a Kurdish boy from Holloway, North London seemed equally mystified:

> 'I don't know why we have to do French. There aren't any French people where I live. There's now plenty of Polish. Why French? I've only heard of Thierry Henry and now he's gone to Barcelona.'

Although the National Curriculum has become less ethnocentric over the years, some continue to say it still does not truly reflect the multicultural make-up of the

UK. Why, for example, are the modern foreign languages taught almost always European ones?

The introduction of Citizenship into the National Curriculum is what pupils would see as topics covered in PSHCE, RE and tutorial work. Students do see the importance and relevance of this area of the curriculum. They identify aspects of Citizenship as having social responsibilities and showing care and consideration for other people and groups. They see its importance as allowing them to discuss and hear about issues that will enable them to become responsible members of society. In tandem with the pupils' general comments about PSHCE, the success and quality of Citizenship teaching and learning depend upon teacher confidence, expertise and the availability of resources. Like all areas of the National Curriculum there are some topics well received and others less so.

A bright Year 11 boy, born in the UK and whose parents were originally from Bangladesh, spoke with some confusion about his Citizenship lessons:

> 'We had a lesson about what it means to be British. I was born in Bradford and I suppose that makes me English. Everyone seems to hate the English. The Scots, Welsh and the Irish all hate the English. The north of England don't like the south of England. It seems to me that the English don't like the English. I'm confused. It's probably easier for me to say I'm Bangladeshi.'

Some Year 10 pupils received a seemingly far from stimulating lesson about local government as part of their Citizenship course:

> 'The topic on government we did was dead boring. A councillor spoke to our year in the hall. He was boring and sent us to sleep.'

Another student with a different perspective of the same talk played devil's advocate:

> 'Yes, he was not the most inspiring of speakers. I felt sorry for him. It was not the most inspiring of topics either and he did lose the plot at times. It's a good job we're not examined on this work.'

The same criticism of the credibility of Citizenship has been levelled at PSHCE topics for years. If the pupils see it as being non-examinable then it doesn't have the same credence as other areas of the curriculum.

Pursuing the subject of PSHCE, I was told of a Year 11 girl, Jasmine Golightly, who was notorious for telling it like it is. She added her two ha'p'orth about the school's sex and relationships education in PSHCE:

> 'Our sex education lessons are really good and cover all sorts of things. Miss never gets embarrassed about anything. I told Miss she ought to include a lesson on how to deal with the leching of that new randy male PE teacher. I've never seen Miss blush before but she did then.'

The way the primary–secondary transfer process operates between schools can impact upon pupil performance at the start of their secondary school lives. In terms of the way the curriculum is delivered many schools continue to go their own sweet way and this leads to a lack of continuity of learning. In 2003 the NFER (National Foundation for Education Research) found that 40 per cent of pupils lose motivation and make no progress at all after transferring to secondary school. One principal reason for this seems to be that the primary schools push Year 6 pupils hard using SATs practice tests and by running booster classes. This intensive pressure and period of high focus can lead to pupils feeling a lack of challenge in Year 7. By the end of this inception year, enjoyment and achievement starts to idle.

Transition from Key Stage 3 to Key Stage 4 is seen by pupils as a momentous change on a par with primary–secondary transfer. Making this change as smooth as possible and giving pupils an understanding of their new curriculum diet is seen as a priority. Students spoke positively about the preparation work undertaken by their Year Managers and subject teachers. One Year 10 boy pointed to subject taster sessions as being a valuable effort made by the school, particularly for new additions to the curriculum:

> 'On the option sheets were new subjects like Media Studies and Business Studies. We could read about them in the option booklet but being able to attend sample lessons helped you in making choices.'

Another student, however, whose perspective on life in Key Stage 4 contained more jaundice than a hospital liver unit, reflected:

> 'It was all show in that talk we had. She wanted people to opt for her subject. Having done it for two terms it ain't that glamorous, I can tell you!'

Many students will be mature enough to sort things out for themselves and value subject handbooks, school options meetings and the talks given by subject staff. Some students will openly talk about the influence of their parents in making curriculum decisions. Some of the information received from home can sometimes be erroneous or a trifle confused. One parent, clearly from a different epoch, questioned why Latin was not on the curriculum because she wanted her daughter to study medicine. Another couldn't understand why PE was being offered at GCSE and why wasn't it compulsory for everyone in this age of obesity?

Coping with the demands of these GCSE courses seems to produce similar responses from both teachers and their pupils. The quart into a pint pot analogy is frequently used to highlight the pressures exerted upon both parties over a span of five terms. Extensive syllabus material and associated coursework is often affected by projects such as work experience, school entertainment productions and ARDs. There is usually nationwide panic to finish syllabuses, complete coursework and get pupils match fit for the impending public examinations. The students expect this reinforcement and practice time:

> 'I found doing past exam questions very helpful but I felt the lessons we had when the teacher went through the questions with us better than just doing them on our own.'

It's all about the time available for pupils to hone their examination skills. Teachers already feel under enough pressure to get their pupils through the syllabus material and often feel under extra obligation when they hear:

> 'Miss Pilkington gave her group special workbooks which told them what to revise. She also gave them extra lessons in the lunch hour.'
>
> 'Mr Rajani has arranged special revision classes in the half-term holidays.'

Mr Rajani's goodwill was seen by some conscientious and highly organized students as counterproductive:

> 'His extra revision sessions really upset my revision timetable.'

One pupil, clearly feeling concussed by curriculum overload, pointed out to his tutor:

> 'I feel I'm being asked to attend a session after school every day. Last week I was asked to attend two at the same time and I was made to feel really guilty about not turning up for Mrs Goldberg's Geography one. I think teachers should appreciate that other subjects exist!'

GCSE revision is perceived by most pupils as about as appealing as having a boil lanced. To provide anaesthetic for this process a group of pupils felt that one departmental practice was quite refreshing:

> 'Our Science Department rotated teachers in revision lessons so you didn't get the same old stuff from the same teacher. It gave a fresher feeling and livened up the lessons.'

Students seem to be naturally drawn to IT and feel it could be used as an alternative style of lesson and help maintain motivation. One enterprising school set up a series of subject podcasts to help students prepare for exams at their own pace. A major cause for concern with Year 12 and Year 13 students is the use of computer programs to raise their motivation. One rather angry young lady held little faith in their application:

> 'It's often like a script from the TV programme *Little Britain*. I feel I can achieve an A grade, my teacher reckons an A grade is within my grasp . . . but the computer says "No".'

The Bitesize programmes are also spoken about as

helpful and consumer friendly aids to revision. I'm sure parents welcome the positive use of television and computers during examination preparation.

One youngster's Dad, who was a behavioural psychologist, had introduced his wayward son to 'rote learning' to prepare for the public exams. The concept advocates people learning and retaining more using ten-minute bursts of exposure to information followed by ten minutes of relaxation. Unfortunately for our psychology parent, his son filled his days with countless bursts of relaxation and a limited number of ten-minute slots involving factual retention.

One contentious issue that clearly wounds pupils is some adults' open criticism of examination standards:

> 'It seems to me that examinations, in general, are becoming easier.'
>
> 'Examination syllabuses are being dumbed down.'

These are, unfortunately, two common remarks levelled at the quality of our examination system. When such cynicism and ill informed opinion filters through to pupils then it is no wonder they answer such criticism with uncompromising vitriol. A disparaging observation made by a member of the public featured on a television programme which questioned current examination content and standards. The unhelpful comment was met with the following response from an outraged Year 11 pupil:

> 'My GCSE coursework completely removed my social life for over three months. It was like a prison sentence!'

Retaliation towards a rather insensitive uncle, who cast

doubt on the A level experience of today, came from a Year 12 girl:

> 'He ought to try coping with four AS subjects plus coursework and all of my extra curricular commitments. It's supposed to give me what the school calls breadth and balance. He just did three Science A levels in his lower sixth, what a narrow-minded and boring dentist he must be!'

Until the necessary research and findings of the Examination Standards Task Group are made public I feel it wise that everyone with an opinion on such issues should keep it to themselves.

A summary of what the pupils say

1. We feel that all the testing we have to do puts a lot of strain on us.
2. We also feel that our parents and teachers suffer stress over these tests too.
3. Many of us are opposed to league tables. We feel they do not give a true reflection of what a school is like.
4. If these tests are necessary then can someone tell us our results in an easy to understand language.
5. We feel that these written tests are too narrow and they do not examine the many skills we have.
6. We feel we do too much writing and there are too many facts.
7. Sometimes there's too much talk and whiteboard.
8. We want to be able to enjoy our lessons and for them to be more interesting and fun.
9. We'd like the curriculum to be more relevant to our lives.

10 We'd like all schools to help us make the jump from primary school to secondary school a lot easier.
11 If any other adult says examinations are becoming easier, we would like them to try to cope with nine GCSEs and all the coursework that goes with them.
12 We don't really get it. If grades at GCSE go up then people say exams are getting easier. If grades go down then standards are dropping. We find all of this quite insulting.

9 Some pupil centred issues

'Your Mum!'

These two words have more power, more meaning and are more provocative than any other insult known in the world of animal behavioural studies. These words are hurtful, cause distress, pain and anger. A picture of an Inuit in a Geography lesson, a dog skull in a Biology laboratory or a photograph of a homeless person in PSHCE may precipitate the use of these two words by some mindless and irresponsible jester. The thoughtless perpetrator either lights a touchpaper so combustible that a classroom scuffle ensues or occasions a personal wound so deep that the victim experiences a long, miserable and humiliating recovery. These two words are so influential that if, on television, George Bush had pointed to a Tibetan yak and said to Saddam Hussain 'Your Mum!' then the Iraqi retaliation would have been so extreme, we would have soon discovered whether or not he possessed those weapons of mass destruction.

Schools have come a long way in addressing the ubiquitous problems associated with bullying. The Anti-Bullying Charter has been used by many schools as a framework for the development of an anti-bullying policy. The degree of success of this document is rooted in which individuals had leading roles in its compilation. The more successful policies have received input from teachers, non-teaching staff, parents and the student body. Some audacious establishments have empowered the school council to formulate a blueprint of the policy under the watchful eye of Year Managers or a member of the leadership group.

These working parties have sought opinion from the student body through focus teams such as year councils. Some have also used PSHCE and Citizenship lessons to gather ideas. Tutor sessions have been used to canvass opinion by using questionnaires and feedback forms. Students who are normally reluctant to participate in class discussion have been encouraged to use suggestion boxes distributed around the school.

In short, the greater the input of pupil voice into the policy, the stronger the sense of ownership. Pupils feel they have been given an opportunity to explore an important school issue that impacts on them. Their consultation and participation in the formulation of this policy and its acceptance by the Head teacher and governing body will give them greater confidence in the way the school will deal with bullying issues.

Anti-bullying policies will contain information on what a school sees as bullying behaviour. There will be sections on procedures for reporting instances of bullying and information on how bullying will be dealt with by the school. However, in common with all school policies, there must be a monitoring process leading to an annual review and evaluation. The pupil voice will articulate the degree of effectiveness of this policy.

Pupils are pragmatic about bullying. They do see it as unreasonable to expect a large school to be absolutely free from all forms of bullying or for teachers to be able to put a stop to every single episode of bullying as soon as it is revealed. They are, however, the best judges of a school's real commitment and determined approach to tackling bullying and its resolve to ensure that its pupils can learn in a caring and supportive environment.

> 'They get you 'cos you're different. They got me 'cos I'm a mosher. I hate chavs. Five of 'em got me at the bus stop. The Head gave one of 'em three days for giving me a kickin'. Nothing happened to the others but to me they were just as bad. Nothing's changed, they still call me a freak and gob at me.'

Some students feel very strongly that schools can sometimes seem reluctant to involve the police in matters of serious bullying:

> 'This Year 11 nutted me in the playground and broke my nose. He did it when his group nicked our football and I went up to him to get it back. He was showing off to his mates and I got angry and shouted at him and then he nutted me. The school excluded him for a couple of days but that's it. My Mum insisted the school should involve the police because it was a serious assault. The kid hasn't bothered me since but his mates still call me a wanker.'

Bully boxes have been introduced in some schools with mixed success. These boxes are placed around the school whereby pupils can alert staff about problems associated with bullying on paper and post them in the box. A Year 13 girl spoke of this method in her school:

> 'The key to the success or failure of this system lies in teachers being able to distinguish genuine concerns from really malicious or puerile ones. Our school is good at dealing with bullying. Pupils say we have a good pastoral system and in the main they feel confident about talking with teachers, face to face, if they need help. I suppose these boxes may help more timid pupils.'

Pupils speak with confidence and optimism about the use of counsellors who are able to offer students the necessary advice, skills and time to resolve bullying. Church schools may have a chaplain who can take on such an advisory role. Both victims of bullying and the bullies themselves may benefit from their assistance.

> 'In my mate's school they have a trained counsellor who helps in sorting out bullying problems. We don't have owt like that in our school. You see your tutor or Head of Year.'

Counselling is extremely time consuming and pastoral figures in schools already have overloaded weekly commitments. The unfortunate position is that there is a lack of suitably trained counsellors in secondary schools.

Some schools use pupils as counselling agents for their fellow members of the school pupil community. There is no doubt about the energy and willingness for students to come to the rescue of their peers. However, they feel that if they are asked to take on such a responsible role they need substantial training. As one Year 11 girl put it:

> 'It's a good idea in theory and our school has tried it. The students who wanted to get involved were given a number of talks by the Deputy Head and a few practice situations to deal with. However, I'm still not sure I'm totally confident about dealing with some things. I mean, if it's hard for adults to sort out bullying, it's going to be even harder for us, I think.'

A Year 11 boy thought the pilot scheme in his school was an extremely brave undertaking but added the caveat:

> 'I would feel a little uneasy about things. I would be worried about giving the wrong advice and messing the whole thing up or even the parents suing me!'

A Year 12 girl had similar reservations:

> 'I know we are told that if things start getting too heavy with what the pupil tells us we are to report it to our supervisory teacher but I'm just a little worried about the responsibility. A girl in my year group self-harms. If anyone told me something like that in our talks I'd panic.'

Many students see the value of peer mentoring but share some doubts and pessimism about many aspects of peer counselling. Similar reactions were gleaned about the concept of bully courts whereby pupils should sit in judgement on their peers and subsequently decide upon the punishment of the bullies. A Year 9 who spoke with a confidence and clarity not too dissimilar to Demosthenes said:

> 'Bully courts! I think they're a monstrous idea. I'm all for pupil involvement in school matters but this is just too extreme and progressive. No thanks!'

Another member of his year, but unfortunately with a contrasting humanitarian perspective, offered the following submission:

> 'If anyone bullied me I'd get 'em permanently excluded and sent to a young offenders unit. I'm like me Dad, I'd have 'em whipped as well!'

For the record, Judge Jeffreys is alive and well and lives in a suburb of Sheffield.

A few schools have also tried somewhat innovative tactics for dealing with bullying such as 'shared concern', 'no blame' and 'solution focused approaches'. The 'shared concern' and 'no blame' prescriptions are similar mechanisms and both have been criticized for failing to allocate blame and aiming for bullies to be able to accept responsibility for their actions and cease forthwith the bulling behaviour. Both systems are very time consuming but as one pupil commented:

> 'If our school has the expertise to follow these techniques then do it. Anything is worth considering when it comes to solving bullying.'

The 'solution focused' method avoids delving into the complex relationship problems that can give rise to some perceptions of bullying. Finding a solution without dissecting out a maze of personal relationship issues is less time consuming but frequently avoids truly addressing the problem.

> 'I did what we'd been told. I spoke to a teacher. I went to my Head of Year. He said something like this is a matter for me and Rachel to sort out. Meanwhile if we had nothing good to say about each other then stay away from each other. I just felt he was too busy to be really bothered and just wanted a quick fix.'

Mediation services will form part of any recommendation programme for dealing with bullying. Heads of Year and tutors very often play a key role in the resolution process. Learning Support Assistants and even pupils themselves can act as this third party. Mediation again is often a protracted affair and as one bully boasted to his friends:

> 'I'm not bothering with that. He's in the wrong and not me.'

As the victim reported to the mediator:

> 'I'm not negotiating this. He was in the wrong and not me.'

Pupils expect instances of bullying to be recorded. It reassures them not only that the matter has been taken seriously but also that something will be done about it. Recording bullying incidents can help teachers look for patterns and ensure matters are not overlooked. A Year 7 reflected on his Key Stage 2 experience:

> 'At our primary school our Head teacher put in a book when someone was bullied. I was a bit disappointed, though, when I told my class teacher about some girls that had picked on me and she just told me to stop telling tales.'

One school council recommended the use of a 'safe room' as a form of sanctuary for pupils who may need temporary respite from bullying or associated issues. It was to be used at break and lunchtimes. There were perceived short-term advantages to establishing such a facility but one student council member acknowledged:

> 'I think there's a danger that some pupils may get too dependent on this room. It may alienate them if they used it too often and do nothing for their confidence with other pupils. I feel the use of the room should be monitored by a teacher.'

The above would suggest a future Head teacher in the making.

Bullying can manifest itself in different ways, from the overt physical forms such as hitting, kicking and even theft, to the more subtle and indirect examples of rumour spreading and exclusion from social groups. Verbal bullying will include name calling, racist remarks, homophobic comments and the now all-too-common cyber-bullying which cut across all forms of covert bullying.

Whatever the instance, pupils expect the school to do

something about the problem and a clear message given to perpetrators that it will not be tolerated. Punitive measures and advice on preventative strategies for avoiding future bullying is much valued by pupils along with a reassurance that there will be continual support to restore their confidence, dignity and self-esteem.

*

> 'We looked like nuns. Black blazer, black jumper, black skirt, black tights and black shoes. We roasted in the summer.'

I distinctly remember this complaint from a Year 11 girl who attended a school where its uniform regulations, like many other of its rules, seemed both outdated and draconian. Things finally changed when the Head teacher, who displayed all the sympathy and understanding of a Khmer Rouge brigadier, finally retired and then concentrated on persecuting his wife and family. His replacement was a more liberal and egalitarian lady, who quickly changed the habits of a lifetime, if you'll pardon the pun.

School uniform policy is supposed to support the school ethos, encourage a sense of identity and belonging, allow equality of dress and avoid fashion competition pressures. Uniforms can be as detailed and specific as that worn by a Grenadier guardsman or as flexible as a simple colour scheme. One lunchtime on a non-uniform day, I gazed across a playground flooded with a sea of denim, trainers and T-shirts and a perceptive Year 10 boy remarked:

> 'It's amazing, Sir. We've just swapped one uniform for another.'

One recent change in uniform policy for many schools is

an equal opportunity issue allowing girls to wear trousers. Pressure from school councils has been instrumental in effecting this change. One ageing Head teacher told me:

> 'Their argument for this change was delivered to the governing body in such a mature and convincing way, we could not turn down their request. All credit to them. A school council going about things the right way.'

Similarly, I once presided over a school council meeting where PE clothing was on the agenda. The boys were complaining about regulation school swimming trunks. Not belonging to the Physical Education fraternity, I was unaware of their enforced aquatic garment. The trunks did look hideous, almost resembling loincloths, and left the boys looking as though they were auditioning for 'Joseph'. Their request was granted. They also played a key role in selecting the new style. As one boy put it:

> 'Just 'cos you do something for forty years doesn't always mean it's right, does it, Sir?'

Students feel that any school policy should be both clear and consistent. Uniform policy should be no different. It is, therefore, an injustice when some students are treated differently by teaching staff.

> 'I got sat outside Miss Chopra's room all day with set work when I came in with trainers. I saw this kid in another year going to normal lessons and he was wearing trainers as well.'

Parents sign up to the home–school agreement before they send their child to the school. The school feels they should receive support and backing from parents if their child fails to comply with the uniform regulations. Sadly, this does not always happen. As one surly mother commented:

> 'He goes out after me. I can't be there to make sure he got his uniform on so don't go ringing me up. It ain't my fault.'

Problems with jewellery can be a time consuming chore for teaching staff. Students will frequently find some way to challenge the uniform policy. As body piercing has become more accessible to youngsters so the problems have increased. At one time, some schools chose to allow ear studs and not earrings. Having thought that was the end of things they were suddenly faced with judgements on navel, tongue and eyebrow jewellery not to mention rulings on tattoos and hairstyles. A rather unpleasant Year 9 pupil, with all the appeal of *C. difficile*, told his tutor:

> 'You see, Miss, I just like to push it as much as I can. They can't permanently exclude me for uniform things. Let 'em try.'

Another Year 11 student complained about victimization and being sent home for sporting bold, red streaks in his hair:

> 'There are some geeks and Goths with jet black hair. They haven't been given a hard time. They should make it clear in the rules and say no dyeing of hair. Mind you, my Dad says they'd have to send half the teachers who are over fifty home.'

*

Chat with any Year 7 pupil early in the autumn term and you will hear similar stories. The primary–secondary transfer can be a frightening and possibly an intimidating experience. In many ways some students will experience a feeling of bereavement when they change schools. A Year 6 teacher explained:

> 'We always get quite a number of pupils coming back to see us at the first possible moment. It must be a shock to the system when they have to move to the big school even though we try to prepare them for the hop as much as possible. It's an insecurity thing.'

If pupils attend a secondary school different to their friends' this too may lead to feelings of loss and isolation. The majority of schools want to keep friendship groups together or pupils from the same feeder schools in the same tutor group.

> 'I was glad to be with Alex. She wasn't a close friend at my primary school but it was good to have someone I knew. One girl in my form didn't know anyone and at lunchtime she started to eat her sandwiches on her own so we sat next to her.'

Pupils must shoulder significant changes. The immediate difference is one of size of their new school. They have more than one classroom. The layout of these classrooms is different. They have a number of teachers rather than the familiarity of just one or two teachers. There are different teaching styles and they are forced to sit in one place more than they have previously experienced.

> 'Moving from one room to another is not something that happened in the juniors. There was no real place for you to call your own.'

> 'It wasn't just the lessons that worried me. It was the new journey to school. I had to get used to catching two buses. My primary school was only down the road.'

> 'Someone told me we have to dissect an eye in Science in our first term. I didn't look forward to that.'

Transfer schemes have improved considerably with all secondary schools employing taster days or induction sessions for their new flock. The quality and degree of commitment of these schools to Year 7 inception does vary. A Year 7 girl spoke in praise of her new school:

> 'Before we visited our new school we were able to use video conferencing to speak with some of our new teachers and they answered lots of our questions. We felt as though we knew them when we came for our big school visit in July.'

Another Year 7 from a different school was also quick to congratulate the efforts made by her current school:

> 'We were asked if we wanted an e-buddy. This was a Year 7 pupil who had already done a year at the big school and someone we could email about any worries or problems we had before we moved to the new school. It was good to talk to someone who knows exactly how we feel and no, we don't have to dissect an eyeball in our first term.'

It is readily acknowledged that a secondary school with a large number of feeder schools has a much more uphill challenge in primary–secondary transfer than neighbourhood schools fed by three or four primaries. One principal concern of primary teachers is the change in curriculum and teaching methods. A Year 6 teacher of many years confessed:

> 'In our borough we are supposed to use a transfer curriculum in Maths and English. We very rarely see a secondary teacher. We have to visit them. I feel it would be helpful if they reciprocated and spent the day with us to see how we do things and what the children are used to.'

Ofsted reports a worrying anaemic continuity of learning between many primary and secondary schools. A pupil in Year 8 remembered an integrated studies project jointly run by her primary and secondary school as a bridging curriculum:

> 'It was great because we just continued what we had been learning with our Year 6 teacher. We had the same teacher for English, History and Geography. I felt it helped us settle in easier than my mate at another school.'

*

If there is one topic that appears on the agenda of all school councils it is toilets. Many groups have urged their school to accept a School Toilet Charter. The rationale behind such a contract was clearly summarized by a Year 11 girl:

> 'When I go shopping to Lakeside [a large shopping complex in Essex], the public toilets are cleaned more than once a day. There's never a shortage of loo paper and there are hygienic sanitary bins in every cubicle. The toilets are nicely decorated. It's just quite civilized.'

A fellow school council member spoke for the male gender:

> 'Toilet seats are always in place too and there's always soap and something to dry your hands. I also feel there should be privacy partitions between the urinals. We are not

> asking for the earth. Some of the things we have to put up with are quite inhuman.'

It was clear that pupils wanted the opportunity to tackle their peers about toilet issues and for their requests not to appear unilateral. A student team saw their Head teacher and his reasoned response was:

> 'Well, you've asked for me to do things concerning toilet improvements. Now what are you going to do about it?'

One female spokesperson said the Head was quite surprised when she immediately replied:

> 'We want to talk about toilet issues in assemblies, tutor time, PSHCE and Citizenship lessons. Pupils are more likely to listen to each other than to teachers. Some of the members of our school need reminding about basic things like the need for flushing the loo and the importance of washing your hands. It's surely part of the Healthy Schools Programme?'

Another student council was pleased with their school's response to concerns over toilets. They explained about not only the need to refurbish their toilets but also the fact that there was nowhere for the pupils to 'hang around' on cold and wet days. It was the sensible way they went about the problem that impressed their Head teacher. Their recommendations and requests were seen as reasonable and achievable. Subsequent change came about with the two parties working cooperatively.

*

A former colleague once described the compilation of the school timetable as like solving a giant Sudoku. The timetable has power and can determine many things about school life. I have known timetablers so glad to put the final touches to their masterpiece that anything will do. Their frustration, exhaustion and lack of patience forced them to complete their jigsaw by cutting surfaces off the final pieces and hammering them into place to make them fit. Such desperate action is not good for anyone on the receiving end of the school day. A good timetabler can enhance teaching and learning and influence movement about the school.

Pupils have their own take on living the school day. Some point out the massive overcrowding on staircases at lesson changeover times. Other groups complain that there is no changeover time between lessons and how impossible it is to get to a lesson on time. One particular school with obvious discipline problems at lunchtimes had shortened their break to such a degree that pupils barely had time to play. Twenty-minute games of football were being played by sandwich eating, coke swigging and crisp chomping participants with mouths so bloated with food they couldn't shout 'Goal!!'

Another school had extremely narrow corridors flanked with lockers. One pupil described lesson changeovers as like a potholing exercise. Student council pressure forced the 'powers that be' to take a closer look at pupil movement around the school and decided on a one-way system that had a most welcome effect on relieving congestion.

> 'One thing that bothers us is those mobile classrooms. Why they call them mobile I don't know. They've never moved all the six years I've been here. They're awful. No soundproofing and freezing cold in winter, baking in the summer. My friend has one of these rooms as his tutor room and saw someone rock backwards on his chair and nearly go through the wall.'

Teachers complain when they do not have a classroom as a base. Their moans are quite justified for many reasons. Pupils too would prefer a subject lesson to take place in the same room.

> 'It's not possible to put examples of our work on the classroom walls and we're never quite sure where the textbooks are. My teacher always asks one of the class to go and get our exercise books from the staffroom 'cos he's not got his own teaching room.'
>
> 'We have History three times a week and each lesson is in a different room. One of them is in the back of the hall. We don't like it and neither does Miss.'

Whatever the structure of the school day there should always be a balance between learning, eating and recreation times. One Year 9 member complained about his hunger, which reaches a crescendo at morning break:

> 'It's just too long to go without food. I've never eaten much breakfast, I just can't force it down. When it gets to morning break, everyone's starving especially those of us who have to get up very early because we live a long way from school.'

The theory that youngsters learn and behave better in a morning has made some schools arrange the structure of their school day accordingly. The same, of course, applies to teachers. They are generally fresher a.m. rather than p.m. unless you are talking about some young staff who start their weekends on Thursday evenings. Friday mornings for them are moribund experiences.

Mornings have thus become longer and lunchtimes displaced into the start of the afternoon. These changes must embrace the work–eating–play ideal for them to be successful. One Year 11 girl commented:

> 'These changes in the school day don't really bother me. Some people have complained about morning break but I mean, I don't live to eat.'

A Year 8 insulin-dependent diabetic boy had the opposite perspective, of course, and said:

> 'I have to eat to live.'

A summary of what the pupils say

1. If we haven't already been involved in writing the school's anti-bullying policy then we'd like to play a major part in its review and evaluation.
2. A school's anti-bullying policy should possess both proactive and reactive strategies. It should be easy to understand and free from jargon.
3. The policy will focus on both victim and bully and any sanctions or ways of punishing bullying should be clear and consistent.
4. We want bullying behaviour to feature in PSHCE and Citizenship lessons.
5. We'd like all schools to be subjected to care and welfare inspections and that these inspections could take place unannounced.
6. We'd like all reported bullying incidents to be recorded on file.
7. We'd like the possibility of bully boxes being used as one means of reporting bullying.
8. We are uncertain about using pupils as counsellors. We feel there needs to be closer supervision and

tighter control if a school does pursue peer counselling.

9 We'd like a school to have its own professional counsellor.
10 We'd like schools to investigate the possibility of using 'safe rooms'.
11 We'd like school council to form part of any review of the school uniform policy.
12 We'd like the school to be consistent in its approach to dealing with breaches of uniform regulations.
13 We'd like the home–school agreement to be reviewed from time to time.
14 To help pupils and their Year 6 teachers we feel it is important that secondary school subject teachers visit our primary schools more often to see how we are taught and learn.
15 Can new technology, for example video conferencing and emailing, be used in helping the primary–secondary transfer?
16 Can schools investigate a bridging curriculum to help the Year 6 to 7 transfer?
17 We'd like all schools to sign up to a Toilet Charter that gives pupils and teachers fundamental rights to demand clean, hygienic and well-maintained toilets.
18 We'd like to see toileting feature as part of healthy schools education in PSHCE and Citizenship lessons.
19 Could those people responsible for producing the school timetable and the structure of the school day listen to any comments or criticisms from the student body? Any recommendations are to benefit both pupils and the teachers.

10 Some final words

I recall driving to school one winter's morning and observing some fresh graffiti daubed on the rear wall of one of the mobile classrooms. It read:

> 'Lafferty is a bastard.'

I instantly knew the person responsible for such words. I knew it was Frank Dunn. Tyrone Lafferty of Year 10 was, indeed, an odious individual. Poor old Frank, a music teacher for many years, had obviously experienced such a bad time with Tyrone the day before, he had decided to let the world know of his personal contempt for this pupil. I would not recommend such a therapeutic response to experiencing bad days with youngsters. It will have a sudden effect on your teaching career. Career is, perhaps, the appropriate word as you watch your job, mortgage and pension move downhill at great speed.

Kids will wind you up. It's part of their job description. It's because of this, and the fact that teachers have been given more work to do than ever before, that we sometimes take a rather blinkered and unenthusiastic view about pupil participation in appraising school related issues. Major organizations nowadays see the value of consulting their customers in order that they may improve the quality of the services they provide. Schools should be no different. Pupil voice is their parallel.

Pupil voice should be used as one of several

indispensable agents in any school auditing its pastoral, teaching and organizational practices. Schools are reporting successes in this consultation process and are convinced that listening to students is one essential vehicle for improving their schools. I recall one teenage curmudgeon, grumbling in the early days of school councils:

> 'If you consulted us more then maybe we'd cooperate and learn more.'

The above remark was hardly dressed with diplomatic verbiage and tact but nevertheless expressed the raw feelings of a school population previously excluded from the participation process.

Pupils do not want to be granted absolute omnipotence in the way their schools are run. While they applaud the principles of democracy and consultation they do, in fact, feel a sense of security with the traditional pupil–teacher ascendancy. Indeed, many pupils say they would feel uncomfortable with revolutionary regimes such as the 'free range' style of education and self-governance as practised at A. S. Neill's Summerhill School.

Pupil voice is not a threatening venture. It should not be viewed with trepidation and impending doom. There is much we can learn from our classroom allies.

As a postscript to the Frank Dunn experience, he was in the school car park a couple of days later, attempting to start his car. His efforts were sadly in vain. This would complete Frank's week.

> 'Try sticking it in gear and rocking it!' came a cry from a passing pupil.

It was Abdul Freeman, a Year 10 boy and Lafferty acolyte. Abdul was a lairy fellow, expected to secure only an ASBO as the sole qualification for his CV.

> 'Go on, Sir. Your starter motor sounds jammed,' persisted Abdul.

He then came over, put the car in gear and proceeded to shake Frank's car with frightening power. He took the keys, started the car and said:

> 'There y'are, Sir. Always does the trick but I'd get it looked at 'cos it'll do it again.'

He then shook Frank's hand, shouted to a couple of his mates then ran off to have a spliff on the way home.

Never underestimate kids.

Bibliography

Apple, M. and Beane, J. A. (eds) (1999) *Democratic Schools: Lessons from the Chalk Face*. Buckingham: Open University Press.

Arnot, M., McIntyre, D., Pedder, D. and Reay, D. (2003) *Consultation in the Classroom: Developing Dialogue about Teaching and Learning.* Cambridge: Pearson Publishing.

Blishen, E. (1969) *The School that I'd Like*. Harmondsworth: Penguin.

Bryson, N. (1995) *Looking at the Overlooked*. London: Reaktion Books.

Cullingford, C. (1991) *The Inner World of the School: Children's Ideas about Schools.* London: Cassell.

Flutter, J. and Rudduck, J. (2004) *Consulting Pupils: What's in it for Schools?* London: RoutledgeFalmer.

Flutter, J., Rudduck, J., Addams, H., Johnson, M. and Maden, M. (1999) *Improving Learning: The Pupils' Agenda*. Report for secondary schools. Cambridge: Homerton Research Unit.

Goodlad, S. (ed.) (1998) *Mentoring and Tutoring by Students*. London: Kogan Page.

Macbeath, J., Demetriou, H., Rudduck, J. and Myers, K. (2003) *Consulting Pupils: A Toolkit for Teachers.* Cambridge: Pearson Publishing.

Rudduck, J. and Flutter, J. (2004) *How to Improve Your School.* London: Continuum.

Shultz, J. and Cook-Sather, A. (2001) *In Our Own Words: Students' Perspectives on School*. New York: Rowman and Littlefield.

Wyse, D. (2001) 'Felt tip pens and school councils: children's participatory rights in four English schools'. *Children & Society*, 15, 209–18.

Index

Index